Most Wise & Valiant Ladies

MOST WISE & VALIANT LADIES

ANDREA HOPKINS

COLLINS & BROWN

First published in Great Britain in 1997
by Collins & Brown Ltd.
London House
Great Eastern Wharf
Parkgate Road
London SW11 4NQ

1 3 5 7 9 8 6 4 2

A CIP catalogue record of this book is available from the British
Library

ISBN 1 85585 480 5 (hardback edition)

ISBN 1 85585 481 3 (paperback edition)

Editorial Director: Sarah Hoggett
Editor: Susan Martineau
Assistant Editor: Corinne Asghar
Art Director: Roger Bristow
Original Design: David Fordham
DTP Designer: Alison Verity
Picture Research: Philippa Lewis

Colour reproduction: Radstock Repro, Great Britain
Printed in Hong Kong by C & C Offset Printing Co., Ltd.

CONTENTS

❦ INTRODUCTION ❦

> '*...I*T MADE ME wonder how it came about
> that so many men, some of them very
> learned, have been and still are both speaking
> and writing so many wicked insults about
> women and their behaviour ... I began to
> examine my character and behaviour as a
> natural woman, and I also considered other
> women whose company I often kept ... I
> would not see how their claims could be true
> when compared to the natural conduct and
> character of women.'
>
> ❦ CHRISTINE DE PISAN, *The City of Ladies*

Opposite: Joan of Arc – from a sixteenth-century woodcut

WHAT WAS IT LIKE TO BE A WOMAN IN medieval Europe? How did women's experiences, feelings, aspirations and opportunities differ from our own? This book tells the life stories of six women who lived in this exciting period of history. In their own words or in eyewitness accounts, we come face to face with surprisingly intimate and personal accounts of their lives. We think of the Middle Ages as being repressive, but it may surprise to us to learn that women enjoyed more opportunities and suffered from fewer restrictions than in subsequent centuries, until our own. The dominance of men in all active roles, and especially as historians, has, of course, tended to obscure the contribution of women, but recent historical research has made it clear that women formed a vital and active part of society, not only in the traditional roles of cooking, cleaning and child-rearing, but in other work as well.

Medieval Europe, like twentieth-century Europe, inherited a deeply ingrained cultural tradition in which men were seen as more important, more valuable, better than women in every way. They were considered physically stronger, emotionally more stable, intellectually superior and morally less feeble. These ideas were inescapable, part

❧ INTRODUCTION ❧

of the general ideological background. They were endorsed and taught by the Church, which had inherited them from the Hebrew Old Testament, as for example when God tells Eve that 'your desire shall be for your husband, and he shall rule over you' (Genesis 3:16). They were also reinforced by secular taboos and legislation that defined what women could and could not do, but, most importantly, they were drummed into everybody by ceaseless repetition in every kind of literary and oral culture, from minstrels' fabliaux to the theological theses of the mightiest intellectual authorities. But the weight of misogynist tradition and increasingly repressive legislation did not actually succeed in keeping women chained to the kitchen sink (so to speak) until well into what we think of as the modern era. The custom of even the most aristocratic women withdrawing from the table after dinner in order to allow the menfolk to discuss politics and other subjects to which they could not be expected to contribute only came into use in the eighteenth century; it wasn't until the nineteenth century that opportunities for women to live independently reached their lowest level.

What we see in Medieval Europe is that, although, in general, nobody seems to have questioned the universal denigration and subordination of women, their work was essential and respected. Peasant women worked in the fields beside their men, or, if they were lucky enough to be slightly better off, became skilled at the traditionally feminine crafts of spinning, weaving, dyeing and sewing – Joan of Arc was particularly proud of her accomplishments in these areas. The rural economy was essentially underpinned by these activities as well as by all forms of food preparation and preservation. Bourgeois women could and did establish and run their own businesses in towns, as we see Margery Kempe doing before her religious conversion. Women of the landed gentry managed estates, represented their husbands in business negotiations and in court, and deputized for them in every conceivable way, as Margaret Paston did, thus becoming a quite formidable matriarch.

Women of the aristocracy, like Eleanor of Aquitaine, took the opportunity to exercise power on behalf of their husbands and sons but also wielded influence independently. Positions of power and considerable independence could also be attained within the established hierarchy of the Church, as in the case of Hildegard of Bingen. There were also some exceptional women who, gifted with a particular talent, were able to earn their livings as craftswomen; Christine de Pisan was in a position not to have to remarry or enter a religious order after her husband's death. Instead she became a professional author to keep herself and her family.

However, it became much harder for women to forge an independent path after the Renaissance as a result of a general tightening-up of the hold on status and power by the male establishment throughout Europe. It became more difficult for the have-nots to have anything at all and women suffered along with the lower classes, excluded from education and opportunities for advancement.

There are many excellent general books available about women's lives and experiences in the Middle Ages. This book focuses on the life stories of six remarkable women, each of whom came from a fairly typical background, but who were able to achieve an extraordinary amount. The six women featured here range from the very famous – everyone has heard of Joan of Arc – to the relatively obscure – Margery Kempe and Margaret Paston.

These six women were chosen for two reasons. The first is that they represent every social class. Although Joan of Arc could not be described as typical of French peasant women, her background and upbringing speak through her recorded words; illiterate but proud of her manual skills, having a limited vocabulary but full of vigorous common sense. The second reason is that, with the exception of Eleanor of Aquitaine, each of these women has left us a personal testament of her own experiences in her own words, and these are fascinating stories, quite apart from their historical significance.

Ultimately, the interest for the general reader is in the recognizable identity and character of a fellow human voice, with whom we can sympathize (or not). Our understanding of the unique and distinctive experiences of one individual is more important than a history lesson, although the medieval period, at once bizarrely alien and breathtakingly familiar, contributes greatly to the stories. And what stories!

Joan of Arc single-handedly turned the tide of a war in stalemate to the favour of the French, soaring rapidly from obscure peasant girl to adored holy warrior maiden before her failure, betrayal and terrible death. Eleanor of Aquitaine, one of the greatest heiresses in history, was Queen of France at fifteen and Queen of England at thirty. She divorced her first husband, a dreadful scandal, and was patron to wonderful poets. A highly political and influential player, her life is too sensational for fiction. Hildegard of Bingen, an amazingly talented woman whose achievements ranged from the creation of exquisitely beautiful choral music to an acutely observed and insightful treatise on human life and our place in the greater scheme of things. She claimed such authority for herself that she was able to admonish and advise kings, emperors and popes. Margery Kempe, who travelled the length and breadth of medieval Europe on pilgrimage, and boldly asserted her right to worship God in her own highly individual way. Margaret Paston, who exemplified the professional wife in the later medieval period with astounding energy and courage. Christine de Pisan, who won her financial independence by pursuing a career as a professional author, and who defended the female sex against the established view of them as weak and vicious, becoming the first consciously feminist voice of modern Europe. It is fascinating to read their stories, but even more so to hear their voices, to make their acquaintance through their own words. In some ways we feel as if a great, unbridgeable gulf separates us from the medieval world, but the details of their lives bring the past vividly to us and, like the sound of a familiar step or a certain smell that reminds us of a familiar scene, these stories evoke our common humanity, our shared experiences of life.

– I –
❦ JOAN of ARC ❦.
c. 1412-1431

> '*T*HEY TIED HER TO a stake ... and lit the fire under her. She was soon dead and her clothes were burned away; then they raked back the fire and showed her naked body to all the people so that they could see the secret parts that belong to a woman, and there were no doubts in their minds. When they had stared long enough at her dead corpse tied to the stake, the executioner got a big fire going again around her poor carcass and it was soon burned up, both flesh and bone reduced to ashes.'
>
> ❦. LE BOURGEOIS DE PARIS *A Parisian Journal*
> TRANS. J. SHIRLEY, (OXFORD 1968)

Opposite: A very fine fifteenth-century painting of Joan dressed in armour carrying her sword and her beloved banner, by an unknown artist of the Franco-Flemish school.

THE STORY OF JOAN OF ARC IS SO FAMILIAR to us that it is difficult for us to comprehend how astounding her life was. We will forever think of her as Joan of Arc, instead of Jehanne La Pucelle (the Maid) – which is how she preferred to be known. Joan was not canonized until 1920, and this sparked off a new surge of interest in France's national heroine. A number of influential plays and films have helped to make Joan a household name: George Bernard Shaw's wonderful play *Saint Joan*, and the films *La Passion de Jeanne d'Arc* by Theodore Dreyer (1928), *Joan the Woman* by Cecil B. de Mille (1916), *Joan of Arc* by Victor Fleming (1948) starring Ingrid Bergman as Joan and *Saint Joan* (based on Shaw's play) by Otto Preminger (1957) which starred Jean Seberg. Joan is most famous today for being burned at the stake, and the most powerful image of her is that of a young and beautiful girl, her face rapt and shining with the knowledge of her immortal destiny, about to suffer a cruel death. This has been given all kinds of new resonances by the events of twentieth-century history. But what did Joan of Arc actually do?

Girlhood

We know an extraordinary amount about Joan of Arc. There were three very detailed investigations into her life; the first by a panel of ecclesiastics charged by the Dauphin in 1429, a second at her trial for heresy and witchcraft in 1431 and, the third and most detailed, her posthumous 'rehabilitation' trial in 1455. Of course, all of these had their own agenda; the heresy trial was trying to find evidence to discredit Joan and prove her a liar and a blasphemer, while the rehabilitation trial was blatantly seeking evidence in her favour. Her childhood and upbringing were fairly conventional. She lived in the village of Domremy in Lorraine, which at that time was part of Germany. Her family were reasonably well-to-do free peasants, who lived in a largish stone-built house next to the church, and had their own land and livestock. She had two brothers and a sister, who died young. She told her interrogators that she worked on 'common tasks about the house, only seldom going to the fields with our sheep and other cattle.' Joan's family obviously did not have to send their daughter out into the fields to tend animals, where she might fall easy prey to lustful yokels or, like France's other female patron saint, Geneviève, a passing soldier. Joan was very proud of her traditional womanly skills: 'I fear no woman in Rouen at sewing and spinning.' She did not learn to read or write, but as she put it, 'I learned my faith and was correctly taught to do as a good child should … From my mother I learned the "Our Father" and the "Hail Mary", and the Creed; I had my teaching in the faith from her and from no one else.'

Civil war began in France in 1411, the year before Joan's birth, and continued all through her life. In these war-torn years Domremy was in a dangerous position on the borders of Champagne and Lorraine. Joan grew up keenly aware of the disruption, danger, insecurity and cruelty of the war, and strongly identifying with the French cause. She described how the children of Domremy, which was loyal to the French Crown, would fight battles against the children of the nearby village of Maxey, which was loyal to Burgundy. Factions engaged in war employed mercenary troops to bully and burn towns and villages into submission. La Hire, a commander with whom Joan later fought, was on the side of the French Crown and campaigned in Champagne against villages sympathetic to the Anglo-Burgundian side in the war; his opposite number, Robert de Saarbruck, rampaged around Domremy and in 1423, when Joan was about eleven, forced Domremy to pay taxes to him. In 1428, when Joan was sixteen, another Burgundian, the Governor of Champagne, Antoine de Vergy, attacked the local administrative centre, Vaucouleurs, during the course of which he burned Domremy and the surrounding villages to the ground. The village was evacuated, and Joan was sent to stay 'for fear of the Burgundians … in the town of Neufchâteau in Lorraine…and I stayed there for two weeks.'

A medieval woman preparing food. Even though we think of her as a great warrior, Joan was very proud of her traditional womanly skills.

She explained that although she did not usually look after the animals, 'I used sometimes to help take them to pasture, or to a castle called the Island, when there was fear of soldiers'.

She was very religious. She went to confession and received the Eucharist once a year from her parish priest, which was the norm for that time, but she loved the legends of the saints and was much fonder than her friends of acts of personal devotion such as prayers and fasting. However, all the witnesses at her rehabilitation testified that she was a strong, healthy, robust girl, not at all hysterical or whimsical or given to unhealthy obsessive kinds of religious practice.

Joan's Voices

Joan was convinced that she had been appointed by God to perform specific tasks, and this enabled her to achieve so much. She testified that she had been receiving divine revelations since the age of thirteen:

Woodcut of a female saint. Joan was familiar with the tales of the saints. She claimed to receive divine visions, especially from Saint Catherine.

> *When I was thirteen, I had a voice from God to help me govern myself. The first time, I was terrified. The voice came to me about noon;...I had not fasted the day before. I heard the voice from my right, coming from the church. There was a great light all around.*

When Joan was first questioned about the voices at her heresy trial in 1431, she described hearing just one voice, emanating from a bright light. This she referred to as her 'counsel', without giving it a name or identifying it with a particular saint This is an experience very similar to that reported by other mystics in the Middle Ages, for example Hildegard of Bingen's 'living light' or Saint Teresa of Avila's divine radiance. For Joan, too, the light was always accompanied by a voice:

> *Two or three times a week the voice told me that I must depart and go to France ... and the voice said that I would raise the siege before Orleans; it told me to go to Vaucouleurs, to Robert de Baudricourt, the captain of the town, who would give me men to go with me. And I answered the voice that I was only a poor girl, who knew nothing of riding or fighting.*

But after repeated badgering from her interrogators she began to identify these voices as the Archangel Michael, and Saints Margaret and Catherine. For Joan, it was the message of the voices, rather than who they were, that was important. She gradually came to understand that she had been chosen to be God's instrument in

JOAN
of
☘ ARC ☘

An image of La Pucelle as a peasant girl. It is set within an illuminated inital from a beautiful fifteenth-century manuscript.

saving France from the English, and that she must dedicate her life to this purpose, however ill-equipped for it she felt herself to be. At the age of thirteen she made a vow of chastity, a state which was more significant then than now, and which was to have profound consequences for her future treatment. This was not unusual for bourgeois and gentry women, but such a vow was unusual for a working woman who in the normal course of things would marry and raise children.

At the fourth session of her trial, Joan suddenly revealed that the first voice was Saint Michael, who prepared her for future visits from Saint Margaret and Saint Catherine. They explained to her 'the pitiable state of the Kingdom of France'.

The Pitiable State of the Kingdom of France

The final phase of the Hundred Years War was a difficult time for the French Crown. King Charles VI of France had become insane in 1392 and thereafter had only brief periods of lucidity. His uncle the Duke of Burgundy and his brother the Duke of Orleans were each as powerful as the King, and their subsequent power struggles made France vulnerable to the English. Henry V's victories were consolidated after his death in 1422 in the name of his infant son Henry VI; the English controlled most of north-western France and much of the South.

By the terms of the Treaty of Troyes, agreed in 1420, King Charles VI and his queen, Isabeau of Bavaria, recognized the son of Henry V and their daughter Catherine as the heir to the throne of France, and disinherited their own son the Dauphin Charles. The wording of the treaty implied that he was illegitimate, and Henry V's propagandists spread rumours that Charles, who had been conceived after the onset of Charles VI's illness, was really the offspring of Isabeau and her husband's brother, Louis of Orleans. Louis was murdered in 1407, hacked to death in the street by the Duke of Burgundy's men as he was returning home from dining with the Queen. This polarized the factions; the Armagnacs, supporters of Orleans, and the Burgundians, and by 1411 the situation had deteriorated into civil war, with the Crown usually identified with the Armagnacs, but both sides making approaches to the English for an alliance.

In 1419 the Dauphin requested a meeting with Duke John the Fearless of Burgundy at Montereau to try to restore peace; but the meeting went horribly wrong. John was killed by an axe-blow to the head before the Dauphin's eyes. This ruined the peace talks, and the new Duke of Burgundy allied himself with the English. By the time Charles VI died in 1422, Isabeau was 'enjoying the protection' of Burgundy, and agreed to declare her son Charles VII illegitimate. Burgundy held Paris, while Charles had a makeshift court and parliament in exile, in towns still loyal to him. When Joan came on the scene, the war was largely a stalemate, but the common people were suffering terribly from the depredations of gangs of soldiers, who were almost worse when unemployed than during a full-scale war.

The Beginning

Joan's mission was not as surprising as we might think to her contemporaries. There was a well-established tradition of (particularly) holy women receiving divine revelations, which often brought them into public prominence. Joan met

This illustration from the Vigiles de Charles VII *by Martial de Paris shows Joan, accompanied by her escort, being led to Charles VII. In fact, by this time Joan had adopted male clothing.*

one such woman but her reaction was hostile, as we shall see later. There were also rumours of a prophecy, that after an evil foreign woman had betrayed France to her enemies (the unspeakable Isabeau), a pure maid from Lorraine would appear and save France. This prophecy was of course much resurrected and discussed after Joan's appearance but she still did not find it easy to gain acceptance. She did not tell her family about her visions for fear that her father would stop her going:

> *When I was still at home with my mother and father, my mother told me*
> *that my father had dreamed that Joan his daughter would leave with a*
> *gang of men-at-arms. This was more than two years after I had first heard*
> *the voices. She also told me that he had said to my brothers, 'If I believed*
> *that what I dreamed about my daughter would come to pass, I would like*
> *you to drown her; and if you did not do so, I would drown her myself.'*
> *...my father and my mother watched me closely and kept me under severe*
> *subjection ... I obeyed them in everything, except my departure ... even if*
> *I had had a hundred fathers and a hundred mothers, and if I had been a*
> *king's daughter, I would still have gone.*

Sculptures from the Palais de Justice at Poitiers. The sculpture above is of Charles VI and the one below shows Isabeau de Bavière.

She knew that her departure had caused pain to her parents, and that 'my father and my mother almost went out of their minds when I left for Vaucouleurs.' When Joan was about sixteen years old, a suitor wanted to marry her, and he gained the support of her father. Joan intended never to marry, and refused him. This brought her into conflict with her father and she was summonsed for breach of promise, and had to attend the Church court at the cathedral of Toul. She was excused because of her vow of chastity, but relations with her father deteriorated, and this may have coincided with Joan's first attempt to leave home and pursue her mission. In May 1428, she persuaded her mother's cousin to take her to Robert de Baudricourt, the governor at Vaucouleurs. Baudricourt was unimpressed and instructed the cousin to take her home with the message that her father should give her a good spanking.

Joan tried again in January 1429. Meanwhile the English had sacked and burned towns and villages in the Meuse valley. Vaucouleurs was the last outpost left loyal to the French Crown. At first Baudricourt refused to see her, but Joan managed to convince two men-at-arms and they persuaded Baudricourt to hear her. In the atmosphere of tension and fear, Joan herself remembered the prophecy about the pure maid from Lorraine who would save France and she identified herself with this magical virgin. Her conviction convinced others. She told de Baudricourt:

> *The Kingdom of France does not belong to the Dauphin but to the Lord*
> *God of Heaven. Our Lord wills that the Dauphin shall be made King,*
> *and have custody of the kingdom...and I shall lead him to his anointing.*

Baudricourt was won over; he gave her a sword, and he also, at her request, gave her the male costume that she was to wear, with one brief exception, till her death. He also provided an escort to take her to Chinon, where the Dauphin's court was residing. The escort consisted of Jean de Metz and Bertrand de Poulengy and four archers. Jean de Metz, a knight, later testified at the rehabilitation hearings that:

> *On the way both Bertrand and I slept every night with her. The Maid slept beside us without removing her doublet or breeches; and as for me, I felt such respect for her that I would not have dared go near her. And I tell you on my oath that I never had any desire or carnal feelings towards her.*

Others also testified to the extraordinary absence of lust that they felt in Joan's company. Joan never explained why she chose to adopt male dress, other than to say that her voices instructed her to do so, and that it was pleasing to God, but it probably made her feel less vulnerable to sexual approaches from her male escorts. De Metz mentioned that she did not remove her clothing at night (though, given that it was February and March, he probably didn't either!)

The journey from Vaucouleurs to Chinon, some 300 miles, part of which was through enemy-held territory, took eleven days. On the way they stopped at the ancient chapel of Sainte Catherine de Fierbois, and Joan spent the day in prayer and heard mass three times. Later, when she was at Chinon, Joan received instructions from her voices, that she would find a sword hidden behind the altar of this chapel. Joan sent word: '... that a search should be made for another sword in the church of Sainte Catherine de Fierbois, behind the altar. It was soon found

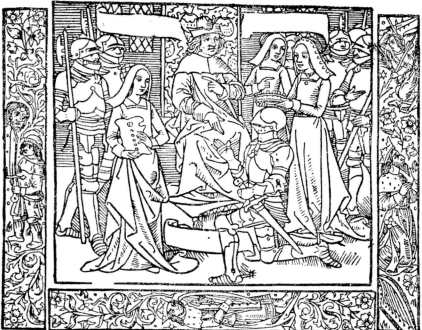

A woodcut from The Vigiles de Charles VII *printed in 1493, entitled 'How La Pucelle Came Before the King'.*

there, all rusted, and on it there were five crosses...I loved that sword, because it was found in the church of Sainte Catherine, whom I loved.'

The party pressed on, meeting with no hindrance. At Chinon there was a delay while the Dauphin decided whether to see her. In the late afternoon she gained admission to his audience chamber, where he was with some of his courtiers. Joan's words about this meeting do not imply, as later story-tellers would have it, that Charles exchanged his clothes with one of them in order to test her, but she does say that her voice told her which one was he, when he was standing with the others:

When I entered the king's chamber, I knew him among the rest, because the voice advised me and revealed it to me. And I told the king that I wanted to wage war against the English.

At the rehabilitation hearing, an eyewitness testified that 'she went up to the king with great humility and simplicity like a poor shepherd girl' and said, 'Most illustrious Sire Dauphin, I have come and God has sent me to bring help to the kingdom and to you.' She herself recalled her message in a more specific manner: 'I bring you news from God, that our Lord will give you back your kingdom, allow you to be crowned at Reims, and drive out your enemies. I am God's messenger in this affair. Set me to work, and I will raise the siege of Orleans.'

It has remained a mystery how Joan managed to convince the Dauphin, who was a distrustful and cynical young man, to take her seriously. At her trial Joan said that she had given the Dauphin a sign by which he knew that she was telling the truth. When questioned on the nature of this sign, Joan eventually came up with a story about an angel appearing and handing Charles a crown. On the morning of her death she is said to have admitted: 'It was I who brought the message of the crown to the king; I was the angel and there was no other. And the crown was no more than the promise of my king's coronation, which I made to him.'

This testimony is not authenticated as the rest of the trial documents are by the signatures of the notaries Boisguillaume and Guillaume Manchon, but the words ring true. Another, and possibly more likely version, is the story told by Charles VII's son Louis XI to the Lord of Boisy, that Joan was able to prove to Charles that she did really have divine revelations because she knew something that no one else could possibly have known – that he had recently, in the castle of Loches, been deeply anxious about the question of his legitimacy, and had got out of bed in the middle of the night to pray on his knees that, if he were not the true heir to his father's throne, he might be allowed to give up the kingdom to the English, put an end to the war, and leave France forever, living out his days in peace. For this to be true, however, we need to believe that Charles was seriously worried, and in the second place, naïve enough to believe that he could simply retire and be left in peace, neither of which is likely. In any case, even if he was illegitimate, it wouldn't make King Henry VI the heir to the throne of France; the next heir would be his cousin Charles, Duke of Orleans, the son of his father's brother Louis.

JOAN
of
❦ ARC ❦

Joan in armour carrying her beloved banner, from Antoine de Four's Vie des Femmes Célèbres, *circa 1505.*

What is perhaps more likely is that the politically astute Charles recognized in Joan something that might rally people to his cause and dynamize the war effort. She was not like other visionaries. She spoke very directly and intelligibly. She did not mask her divine message in strange images, but had a list of practical goals to be achieved: raise the siege of Orleans; crown the Dauphin at Reims; liberate Paris; drive the English out. She was undoubtedly impressive, as a prodigy of nature if nothing else; for all her protestations to her voices that she could neither ride nor fight, it appears that she had acquired these skills by the time she reached Chinon. The Duke d'Alençon, one of the Dauphin's most trusted and experienced military commanders, testified at her rehabilitation that at Chinon she had coursed before Charles in the lists, carrying a lance, and that she had handled it so expertly that he gave her a horse. But the ever-cautious Charles had her claims investigated by a tribunal of his parliament in exile. Joan was sent to Poitiers and examined for three weeks by a panel of learned and wily men. They questioned her about her previous life and her divine revelations, and took witnesses as to her character. It was vital to determine that Joan was divinely inspired and not a hoaxer or deluded by the devil. Joan's answers to them, that we know about, show her typically concerned with practical matters. She became impatient when they asked for details about her sign or when they argued with impractical sophistries: 'In God's name, I did not come to Poitiers to give signs! Take me to Orleans...'

The committee at Poitiers declared her genuine. She also submitted to a physical examination to determine whether she really was a virgin. Joan's mission was then officially endorsed by the King's council, and she was given the equipment and following of a knight. She had warhorses (in addition to a black charger already given by the Duke of Lorraine) and ponies, a suit of white armour, weapons, and she had a banner made according to a design dictated to her by her voices which she loved: 'forty times better than my sword'.

She was also given a squire, a page and her own troops. At her trial she said that she had been given command of 10,000 or 12,000 men, but this is either a mistake or an exaggeration; the real number is likely to have been about 300. She was also given beautiful male clothes to wear. At her trial it was claimed that, as well as wearing male clothes, she had also dressed too richly for her lowly rank.

Joan felt confident enough now to send a challenge to the English. She now felt part of the chivalric tradition and the letter she dictated on 22 March 1429, echoes the terms and ideas of chivalry, though not its formal language:

> *Surrender to the Maid, who is sent here by God the King of Heaven, the keys of all the good towns you have captured and destroyed in France...And you should know for sure that the King of Heaven will send more strength to the Maid than you are able to put against her and her good soldiers in any attack. And when the blows begin, it will be clear who is in the right before the God of Heaven...*

This woodcut from the chronicle Vigiles de Charles VII *shows the English laying siege to Orleans.*

The Liberation of Orleans

The English forces were concentrated around the west and south of Orleans – they no longer had enough troops to surround the entire city, but they controlled the most important strategic point – the bridge across the Loire. The French Commander-in-chief, Dunois, was leading his troops to approach Orleans from the undefended north and east, which meant bringing them along the southern bank of the river, crossing it further upstream at Jargeau, and returning along the north bank. Joan, however, had received explicit instructions from her voices that the city should be approached on the north bank, which meant that the French would have to engage the English before they could get into the city. When Joan realized what was happening, she was outraged. To make matters worse, when they arrived at the place where Dunois planned their crossing, they found that the wind was blowing against them and that it would be impossible for them to transport the army and its supplies across the river for the time being, leaving them open to attack. Joan could not contain her indignation. She sought out Dunois (who was the illegitimate half-brother of Charles, Duke of Orleans):

> *Are you the Bastard of Orleans? Was it you who advised that we should come here on this side of the river, instead of going directly to where Talbot and the English are?...In God's name! Our Lord God's counsel is more sure and wise than yours. You thought you had deceived me, but it is yourself you have deceived. For I bring you better help than you could get from any soldier or any city. It is the help of the King of Heaven...*

At this critical moment, Dunois recalled, 'the wind, which had been against us and had absolutely prevented the ships carrying provisions for the city of Orleans from embarking, changed and became favourable.' Dunois regarded this as a miracle and it convinced him of Joan's authenticity. Joan entered Orleans in the evening of 29 April. She was received with joy by the townspeople; they had heard of her mission to raise the siege and already regarded her as their saviour.

Even then, Dunois obviously had reservations about allowing Joan to take part in physical fighting. She made him promise that he would let her know when the English commander should arrive with reinforcements, and she lay down to rest. He did not, and her squire testified that she 'suddenly sprang out of bed and woke me...she said to me, "Ah! you wretch, you didn't tell me that French blood was flowing! ...To horse! To horse! ...in God's name, my counsel has told me that I must attack the English now; but I don't know whether I should go to the fort or against Fastolf, who is bringing them provisions."' She ran out of the tent, jumped onto someone else's horse that was standing outside, and led fresh troops to join the French assault on the English-held Fort Saint Loup.

Joan's arrival was decisive; the fort was overrun and the English retreated. Her first engagement in battle resulted in victory for the French. She was all in favour of aggressive action, and this was often opposed by the real military commanders

The coat of arms granted to Joan's brothers by Charles VII in 1429. This entitled them to use the noble surname 'du Lys'.

JOAN
of
❦ ARC ❧

A miniature from Vigiles de Charles VII. *Joan is offering the keys to the city of Troyes to the King.*

who tended to favour caution. On 4 May there was fierce fighting all day in Orleans; the English had come out of their fortress at the southern end of the bridge, crossed over and attacked the city gate at the other side. The French counter-attacked and chased them back over the bridge, but they turned on the French, inflicting severe losses. The French retreated, but Joan rallied them and inspired them to attack again, so that the English were driven back once more.

Joan did not put on her armour or go out to fight on the following day, because it was the feast of the Ascension; she dictated another letter to the English, warning them to 'abandon your forts and depart into your own country'. The letter was fastened to an arrow and shot into the English camp. Joan was expecting to fight the following day; but the French commanders were again cautious. They wanted to wait for the reinforcements they expected. Joan was bitterly opposed to the waiting game, and urged them to follow up their advantage immediately. She was overruled. On 6 May, she decided to ignore the council's decision and attack anyway. The bailiff of Orleans caught her leading a troop of soldiers out of the south gate and tried to close it against her, but a crowd of enthusiastic townspeople swept her onto the bridge. The English were driven out of the town's Augustinian convent by this attack and lost control of the bridge. Joan, excluded from the council of war with the French commanders, received instructions from her voices, who warned her that she would be wounded the following day 'above the breast'.

On 7 May Dunois led an attack on the fortress of Les Tourelles accompanied by Joan and her men. There was fierce fighting and Joan was struck in the throat by a crossbow bolt. She recalled later: 'I was the first to set a ladder against the fortress on the bridge, and, as I raised it, I was wounded in the throat by a cross-bow bolt.

A fifteenth-century miniature of an exchange of documents between Joan and the King.

But Saint Catherine comforted me greatly; and I did not stop riding and doing my work.' Later on she was obliged to stop riding and rest. A rumour went around that she had been killed; the French soldiers lost heart and the attack began to fail. Dunois was about to call off the attack. Joan, who had pulled the bolt from her wound with her own hands, pleaded with him for one more assault. She went back into the front line, calling encouragement to her soldiers and defiance to the English. She promised that when her banner touched the walls of the fortress, it would fall. Filled with new confidence, the French attacked again, and succeeded in setting fire to the drawbridge and gates of the fortress. Many English soldiers

A rather romantic image of a typical late-medieval walled town, very like the succession of towns in the Loire Valley regained by the French in the summer of 1429.

and knights jumped into the river to escape the fire and drowned. On the following day the English withdrew. Orleans was liberated.

At her trial for heresy Joan claimed that she had never personally killed anyone and that, although she possessed several swords, she always carried her banner when she was leading her troops into battle. She seems therefore to have confined her role to that of a leader who encouraged and inspired her men, but some of the eyewitness accounts from the rehabilitation trial refer to her actively fighting. Whatever the truth was, she led in an active way, displaying enormous courage.

The Summer of Victories

Joan's fame spread, and her mission became a self-fulfilling prophecy. The French fought with new energy and confidence because she had convinced them that God was on their side, while the English were plainly terrified of the Maid's supposed supernatural powers. On 2 June 1429 the King granted Joan the right to arms, and commissioned her and the Duke d'Alençon as commanders of the French forces at the siege of Jargeau – the next town in the Loire valley in English hands. At Jargeau Joan was wounded again but another miraculous-seeming escape made her appear invincible (and aggravated the charges of witchcraft at her trial). Jargeau fell on 11 June. The French moved to Meung and then to Beaugency, where they overcame stiff resistance to take the town.

Joan was upset by all the slaughter. When she saw a French soldier strike an English prisoner on the head and leave him for dead, she comforted the man and heard his last confession. The following day the French won a decisive battle at Patay against the fresh army marched from Paris by the English commanders. Decisively, Joan persuaded the cavalry commander to mount an early charge. Her mere presence was enough to inspire the troops:

> *In God's name, we shall fight them! ... God is sending them to us for us to punish them. Today our noble King shall have the greatest victory he has won in many days...*

Joan was deeply committed to achieving the proper coronation of King Charles VII. It was essential for French monarchs to be crowned at Reims, and to be anointed with the holy chrism (oil) with which St Remy had anointed the first Christian King of the Franks in 490. Reims was in the heart of Anglo-Burgundian territory but Joan begged him to push forward to Reims, and the normally cautious Charles mounted a campaign, in which Joan and her divine mission assumed a very prominent role. The cities of Troyes, Châlons, and Reims itself, had not been garrisoned with English soldiers because they were considered safely loyal. The citizens of Troyes received one of Joan's letters. They sent out an apocalyptic-preaching friar, Brother Richard to test whether Joan had been sent by God. She recalled with delightful humour how: 'when he came out, he came towards me making the sign of the cross and sprinkling holy water. And I said to him, "Come on bravely, I shan't fly away!"'

Troyes was besieged from 5 to 11 July before it fell. Châlons and Reims followed suit without a

A woodcut from an early sixteenth-century romance showing men-at-arms and soldiers.

blow being struck. From Reims, Joan wrote a letter to the Duke of Burgundy, inviting him to make peace with the King and attend his coronation, adding the warning '...you will win no battles in France against loyal Frenchmen...if you want to make war, go and fight the Saracens'.

The Dauphin was crowned on 17 July. Reims was still behind enemy lines, and the French planned to retreat immediately after the ceremony. It had to be done hastily and without the elegance and display it would have had in peacetime, but the ceremony followed the rite laid down centuries before and conferred on Charles the absolute grace of a consecrated and anointed king. Joan was close to the King during the ceremony.

This was the peak and summit of Joan's fortunes. She had succeeded brilliantly so far in every enterprise and through her influence, through the faith she inspired, she had achieved her first two goals. At the coronation one of the lords in the King's train exclaimed that 'such deeds as you have done were never seen before, nor is anything like them to be read in any book.' Joan replied that her Lord had a book in which no scholar had ever read, be he never so learned.

Decline and Fall

After the coronation Joan was equally urgent that the French should push on to Paris and retake it. However, Charles wanted to withdraw from active warfare, and consolidate his political gains; his first act after the coronation was the symbolic ceremony in which he touched sufferers of The King's Evil, his second to open negotiations with Burgundy for a truce. Under the terms of this truce there would be peace between the French and the Burgundians till Christmas; the Duke of Burgundy would continue to hold Paris unopposed until then; the French could make war on the English without the Burgundians coming to their defence. But very little fighting followed. Meanwhile Charles withdrew himself, his court and his army to the Loire again, and made plans to disband the army for the winter.

A letter dictated by Joan of Arc, dated 9 November 1429.

An illustration showing Joan's unsuccessful attack on Paris on 8 September. This was the feast of the birth of the Virgin Mary, when fighting was forbidden. Joan was criticized for choosing this day and her failure was deeply damaging to her reputation.

Joan was fiercely opposed to this, bewildered and enraged that no one seemed to be listening to her divine mandate any more. She wrote to the citizens of Reims, a letter full of bluster and promises that revealed her pain and confusion. It was a public statement of Joan's disagreement with the King's policy, and an open warning that she might not keep to the terms of the truce; and she didn't. She persuaded some other captains to join her, and on 8 September – the day of Our Lady's Nativity – she attacked Paris, with a small force of a few hundred men. The fact that she had made an attack on a holy day was later brought up against her at her trial, and it does seem to have shocked some of her contemporaries.

Joan expected the citizens of Paris, inspired by the news of her mission, to rise against their oppressors and help her. But they didn't. She mounted an attack on the Porte St Honoré but she was badly wounded again by a crossbow bolt, and was pulled away, protesting that 'the place would have been taken!'. Without her the attack failed; she withdrew and recovered from her wound in a few days; but her reputation as France's invincible saviour had received a fatal blow. She had promised to take Paris as part of her divine mission, and her failure was deeply damaging. Faith in her began to falter. After the King disbanded the army, she needed cash for weapons and provisions and pay for her troops. She took the town of St Pierre le Moustier at the end of October, but had to write a fund-raising letter to the townspeople of Riom:

> *I beg you, if you love the king's well-being and honour, and those of all the others here, to send help for the said siege immediately, of saltpetre powder, sulphur, arrows, heavy arbalests, and other materials of war...*

At this point Joan met a 'visionary' of a much more traditional kind – a young woman named Catherine de la Rochelle. She had been a protégé of Brother Richard, who had so failed to impress Joan before. Catherine claimed divine visions: 'a white lady, dressed in a gown of cloth-of-gold' had told her to travel through all the towns loyal to the King, telling anyone who had gold or silver or treasure stashed away to bring it at once. This treasure, Catherine claimed, was to pay Joan's soldiers with. Joan, sceptical of Catherine's claims, didn't want her help with the fund-raising; she told her to go back to her husband, and attend to her housework and her children. However, Joan was still fascinated by her tales of the 'white lady' that appeared to her. It was reported at the rehabilitation trial how:

> She asked Catherine if her white lady came every night, and, if it were so, she would spend a night with her. And she went to bed with her and stayed awake until midnight; but she saw nothing, and then she fell asleep. In the morning she asked if the lady had come, and Catherine said that she had, but that Joan was asleep and she could not wake her...

Joan concluded from this that Catherine was a charlatan and 'to make sure, I asked St Margaret and St Catherine about her, and they told me that it was all nonsense.'

Brother Richard urged that Catherine's plan should be tried. Part of the reason why Joan did not want to give credence to Catherine was that she was opposed to Joan's plan to besiege La Charité. La Charité was a nearby town held by a freelance *chef de guerre*. In November Joan had failed to take it. In April she fought again at Lagny, and found herself in the strange position of being asked to cure a dying baby. This was a consequence of her fame that always displeased Joan, but when she had made it clear that all she could do was to add her prayers to those of the others, she went: 'and prayed with the others. And at last there were signs of life in him, and he yawned three times. Then he was baptized, and soon afterwards he died and was buried in consecrated ground. They said that for three days he had shown no sign of life, and he was as black as my tunic. But when he yawned his colour began to return.'

She was emphatic that she herself was no supernatural wonder and could not work miracles; at her rehabilitation one of her men-at-arms testified that she was annoyed and upset when some women made as if to worship her.

In May Joan made an attempt to relieve the town of Compiègne, held by the French, but besieged by a combined force of Burgundians, English, and Luxembourgeois. She entered the town in the morning of 24 May and that evening she made a surprise attack with three or four hundred of her soldiers on the Burgundian position. But she had

A woodcut of a typical medieval town showing the town gates.

miscalculated; suddenly the English appeared from the south and the Burgundians from the north, and she and her troops were trapped between the two. Most of her men fled back into Compiègne; Joan could not get away to follow them. The commander of the town had no option but to order the gates closed and the drawbridge raised. Joan was dragged from her horse and taken prisoner, along with her squire Jean d'Aulon, her brother Pierre, and another warrior. Joan, as a valuable prisoner of war, was handed over to the custody of Jean, Prince of Luxembourg. There followed one of the most disgraceful episodes in Joan's story. Jean set her ransom at 10,000 gold crowns, a huge sum of money certainly but one that had been paid before for the release of great lords. But Charles VII made no attempt to pay or to negotiate. Joan's recent failures had cost her dearly; now it was clear that her King felt that she was no longer valuable.

Joan was first held at the castle of Beaulieu, but after a failed escape attempt she was moved to the castle of Beaurevoir near Arras in July 1430. Here Joan was in the custody of Jean's aunt, Jeanne of Luxembourg, and Jean's wife, Jeanne de Béthune. Both of these ladies were rather sympathetic to the French cause, and befriended Joan. She later told her judges that if it had pleased God for her to stop wearing men's clothes, she would sooner have accepted a woman's costume from those ladies than from anyone else in France, except the King's wife. She also said that Jeanne de Luxembourg had begged her nephew not to give Joan to her enemies. But, since the ransom was not going to be paid, the prince could not afford to cross the Duke of Burgundy. The Prince agreed, for the same sum, to

A woodcut showing the English leading La Pucelle to Rouen to be executed.

29

The Duke of Bedford (John of Lancaster) at prayer before St. George. Joan was sold to the Duke by Jean, Prince of Luxembourg.

hand Joan over to the Duke of Bedford, regent to the infant English king.

When Joan learned that she was to be sold to the English she flung herself from the tower of the castle. Severely concussed, she lay for three days without eating or speaking. Gradually she recovered, and in December was transferred to Rouen, where arrangements had been made for her trial.

The Trial

Everything Joan had tried to achieve was within the sphere of military and political goals. However, because she claimed that her actions were in obedience to divine instructions, Bedford had an excellent excuse to have her tried by the Church and interrogated by the Inquisition. She was charged with twenty-four separate counts of heresy, blasphemy, idolatry, and unnatural and immodest behaviour. The day after she was captured a group of churchmen of the University of Paris petitioned the Duke of Burgundy to have Joan tried in this manner; they had a year to think up the charges and plan their attack. Five of the charges concerned themselves with Joan's assumption of male dress, which seems genuinely to have horrified the clerics.

Of course it was much more shocking then than it is now for a young girl to show her legs, but the whole concept of a woman dressing as a man was deeply upsetting to them, against nature and the God-given order of things. But apart from their horror and disgust at Joan's unfeminine dress and behaviour, these clerics committed to the Anglo-Burgundian cause were enraged by Joan's explicit connection of her divine revelations to her political goals. It was completely unthinkable to them that what she claimed could be true – that God was really on the side of the French. It was therefore important to them to discredit Joan, and they concentrated on trying to make it appear that she was either an ingenious hoaxer or an evil sorceress; demonically and not divinely inspired, an object of loathesome impurity and unnaturalness instead of the holy warrior maiden.

The committee of inquisitors and judges were all, of course, loyal to the Anglo-Burgundian cause, and consisted of learned theologians from the University of Paris as well as leading churchmen. The Archbishop of Reims, who had crowned King Charles VII the previous July, took a prominent part in it; the chief judge was the Bishop of Beauvais, Pierre Cauchon. The trial itself was scandalous even at the time for its illegality. Joan had no counsel or legal representation; between interrogation sessions she was kept in a tower room at Rouen Castle, where she was chained to a block of wood at the neck, wrist and ankle. Her warders were five English soldiers who never left her alone and who abused and assaulted her. In court she was continually interrogated by panels of inquisitors, all hostile to her, all well-versed in the skills of dialectic, hoping to trick her into betraying herself.

The trial opened on Wednesday 21 February in the Royal Chapel at Rouen Castle; there were six public sessions, in the chapel or in the Hall of State, followed by ten closed sessions in her prison cell, then further public sessions. For three months the nineteen-year-old Joan was pitted against the combined forces of more than sixty priors, bishops and canons, and it is a great tribute to her that they did not succeed in breaking her spirit until almost the end of that time. Her conduct during this ordeal, which is recorded minutely in the trial documents, was heroic. She spoke with straightforward candour to her accusers, just as she had spoken to dukes and counts at the height of her acclaim. Despite the appalling conditions in which she was kept she refused to be intimidated and answered her interrogators boldly, even contemptuously. The questions she was asked mostly centred on the nature of her voices and the origins of her scandalous male dress. Joan was adamant that she would answer any questions relating to her past and her recent activities, but that there were many things that had been told her by her voices, which were secret and which she had sworn never to reveal. She often refused to answer questions on the grounds that they were irrelevant to the charges. But as time went on she found that she could not evade the constant questioning – how did she perceive her visions – what exactly did she see, what did St Michael, St Catherine and St Margaret look like, what did they tell her? Here, is a passage from the transcript of the fourth public session:

> *Q: Have you talked with St Catherine and St Margaret since Tuesday?*
> *A: Yes, but I do not know the hour.*
> *Q: What day was it?*
> *A: Yesterday and today. There is no day that I do not hear them.*
> *Q: Do you always see them in the same dress?*
> *A: ...I know nothing about their dress.*
> *Q: In what form do you see them?*
> *A: I see their faces.*
> *Q: Do the saints who appear to you have hair?*
> *A: It is well to know they have!*
> *Q: Was their hair long and loose?*
> *A: I don't know. And I don't know whether they seemed to have arms or other limbs. They*

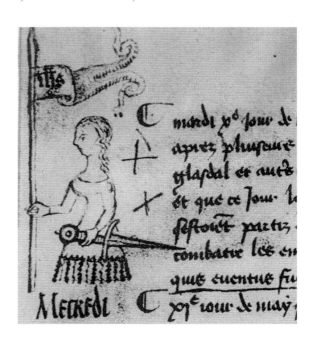

A drawing of Joan 'la Pucelle' doodled in the margin of the register of the Parliament of Paris by the recording of the liberation of Orleans in May 1429. This is the only surviving image of Joan made in her own lifetime. However, the artist had almost certainly never seen her.

JOAN of ❧ ARC ❧

spoke well and beautifully, and I understood them well.

Q: How do they speak if they have no bodies?

A: I leave that to God. They speak in the French tongue.

Q: Does not St Margaret speak English?

A: Why should she speak English when she is not on the English side?

Q: Have the voices told you that you will be freed from prison in three months?

A: That does not concern your trial. But I do not know when I shall be freed. Those who would put me out of this world may well be leaving it before me.

A medieval woodcut of the judges presiding over Joan's trial for heresy.

And so on. In the first sessions, Joan is feisty, confident, even occasionally threatening, as when she tells Pierre Cauchon: 'You say that you are my judge. Think carefully what you are doing, for truly I am sent by God, and you are putting yourself in great danger.' Her voices told her to speak up bravely. When asked if she would like to have female dress, she replied that she would put it on if they would let her go (knowing of course that that was out of the question); otherwise she would keep the clothes she had on 'since it pleases God'. Her conviction of her own rightness never wavered, and at first she did well. But as the days went by she was worn down.

She continued to insist that everything she had done was done by the will of God and in response to direct divine revelations to her, but under repeated questioning in her own prison, in desperation, she did eventually reveal far too much detail about the sign by means of which she had convinced Charles VII of her authenticity. An angel came down from heaven at Chinon, bearing a very rich crown, 'so rich that I could not tell its richness', signifying that he would hold the Kingdom of France. Having squeezed these concrete details of her visions out of her, the interrogators asked her if she would submit herself to the authority of the Church Militant for its judgement on her 'in respect of everything you have done, whether good or evil, and especially in respect of the acts, crimes, and offences with which you are charged'. Joan answered that she would, provided that 'it does not order me to do anything impossible. I call this impossible – that I should revoke the

Joan being tied to the stake. Witnesses said that she did not scream when the fire was lit, but merely prayed to Jesus, Mary and the Saints.

things that I have said and done concerning the visions and revelations I said I had from God. Not for anything will I revoke them.'

Joan continued to insist that her obedience to God must come first, before her allegiance to the Church. The strains to which she had been subjected took their toll and in April she fell ill. Throughout the trial she had begged to be allowed to hear mass, but although she was told that she would be allowed to hear mass if she put on women's clothes, she consistently refused to do so. And she absolutely refused to admit that there was any truth in the charges against her. At last, by 9 May, Pierre Cauchon lost patience and proposed that she should be put to torture. This is what she said: 'Truly, if you were to have me torn limb from limb and send my soul out of my body, I would say nothing else. And if I did say anything else, I would always say afterwards that you had made me say it by force.'

When the matter was put to the vote, the majority of the assembly voted against torture. On 23 May she was again admonished to submit herself to the judgement of the church, i.e. to admit that the charges against her were true. She said:

> If I were at the place of execution, and I saw the fire lighted, and the faggots burning and the executioner ready to build up the fire, and if I were in the fire, even so I would say nothing else, and I would maintain what I have said at this trial until death. I have nothing more to say.

It was truly a Catch 22; the only alternatives before her were to plead guilty as charged - in which case she would be admitting that everything she had said about her divine mission was a lie – or continue insisting stubbornly that she was telling the truth, in which case she would be condemned as an unrepentent heretic. On the following day Joan was taken to the cemetery of St Ouen, where she was publicly

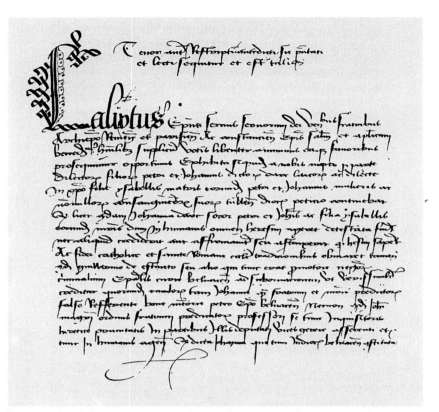

An extract from the Papal Book of Calixtus III ordering a reconsideration of the verdict on Joan's trial.

harangued and the sentence against her read out. From where she stood she could see the mound of faggots around the stake constructed for her execution. Suddenly she asked whether she could submit to the judgement of the Pope. She was told that she could not, and a shortened form of the charges against her was presented to her, which included an admission that she had been 'claiming by lies that I had revelations from God and his angels St Catherine and St Margaret, and all those my words and acts which are against the Church I do repudiate, wishing to remain in union with the Church, never leaving it.' Joan agreed to 'sign' this, saying, 'I would rather sign it than burn.' It seems clear that she believed that if she did this she would be removed from the custody of the English.

Cauchon read out her new sentence, in which she was condemned to life imprisonment 'to be spent in acts of the severest penance'. She seemed almost jubilant after this, and said, 'Now, you men of the Church, take me to your prison, and let me be no longer in the hands of the English.' But, cruelly, Cauchon ordered her to be taken back to the same prison she had come from. Part of her retraction was that she had agreed to wear female clothing. Back in her cell in the castle her head was shaved and she was given women's clothes. But she was left there, with the same five English soldiers, who attacked her and tried to rape her. Fighting them vigorously off, she was badly beaten. She had thought that she would be dedicated to a life of solitude and penitence, but when she realized that she had been tricked, she put her men's clothing back on again. When this was reported to Cauchon, he sent two assessors to question her. She told them that she had recanted for fear of the fire, and that since then her voices had told her 'that I have done and am doing a very great injury to God in saying that what I did was not well done.' She was clear in her mind that her recantation was wrong, so she withdrew it. 'If I say that God sent me, I shall be condemned; but God really did send me.'

This was all Cauchon needed. At nine o'clock in the morning on 30 May, she was dressed in a long white shift and a mitre-shaped hat bearing the words 'Relapsed heretic, apostate, idolater', and taken on a cart to the old market square in Rouen. There a huge and mostly hostile crowd had assembled, and Cauchon read out her final sentence: 'You are for the second time a relapsed heretic; like a dog that habitually returns to its own vomit ... you have fallen back into your former sins ... We cast you out as a rotten member ...'

She was allowed to pray for half an hour. She asked for a crucifix, and an English soldier bound two sticks together and placed it in her hands. She put it inside her shift, and begged that another crucifix be brought and held up where she could see it. She was bound to the stake and the pyre was lit. Eyewitnesses later testified that many of the previously enthusiatic crowd now wept, including the judges.

Other eyewitness accounts agree that Joan lived for over twenty minutes in the fire, and did not scream or groan, but continued to call out to Jesus, Mary and the saints until she died. This made a deep impression on the crowd, and many were convinced that they had killed a genuinely holy woman.

Afterwards

Just over twenty years later the Hundred Years War ended with the Battle of Châtillon; Joan's vision of the English being driven out of France had come true. King Charles opened a new investigation in 1449, with the intention of overturning the trial verdict. It was important to him that someone closely associated with his rise to power should be cleared of the charges of sorcery, heresy, and blasphemy. He had to persuade the Church that there were grounds for overturning the verdict of the previous trial. In November 1455 the official Trial of Rehabilitation opened and took evidence from over 150 witnesses who had known Joan, fought with her, or seen her in action. It found that the previous trial had been invalid on legal grounds, and the Pope formally recognized this in 1456. The cult of Joan grew rapidly and she was seen as a heroine who had single-handedly turned around the French war effort. In the nineteenth century a movement was begun to have her canonized, not for having received revelations – about which the Church remains tactfully quiet – but for her piety, chastity, selfless dedication to God's will, and her bravery in life and in her terrible death. Joan was declared a saint on 9 May 1920 by Pope Benedict XV. Apart from the consideration of her faith, Joan remains an outstanding figure of feminine achievement and a truly inspirational heroine.

que la terre fainte z le prip
ple vpiftiens y demourãt
feuffent fecourus et gardes
contre fes impetueulx affaulx
z leurs trefcinciens et auec
omeiurs. et ouuãt le trefoz
de leglife donna plain pardõ
et remiffion de paine z de
coulpe a tous ceulx a toute
et a ving chafcun de ceulx q

en fauuir et pour aidier la ter
re fainte prendroient lenfeigne
de la fainte Croix z yroient
en celtui vopage. Et combien
quil yeuft lors es diuerfes
parties de vpiftiente plufeurs
feigneurs auteurs z prelats
Toutteffois felon ce que
ieu reuue ieieux comme
leftoure iournal au point du

– II –
❦ ELEANOR of AQUITAINE ❦
1122–1204

'QUEEN ELEANOR, an incomparable
woman, beautiful yet virtuous, powerful yet
modest, unassuming yet eloquent, qualities
that are most rarely encountered in a woman;
still tireless in every undertaking, whose
ability was the admiration of her age ... many
know what I wish none of us had known;
this same queen, in the time of her first
husband, went to Jerusalem. Let no one say
any more about it ... Be silent!'

❦ RICHARD OF DEVIZES, *Chronicle* p.402

Opposite: Saint Bernard of Clairvaux, the most charismatic and influential churchman of the Middle Ages, preaching the Second Crusade in the presence of King louis VII and his wife Queen Eleanor on Easter Sunday, 1146 at the Abbey church of Vézélay.

UNLIKE THE OTHER SUBJECTS OF THIS BOOK, Eleanor of Aquitaine left us no record of her words or deeds written in her own voice. All we know of her comes from the voices of contemporary or later chroniclers, some of whom were extremely hostile to her; so we have to reconstruct from this evidence what kind of a person she was. Fortunately she leaps from the pages of medieval history in vivid life - a vital, even a forceful woman, passionate in her youth, active, dynamic, cultured, beautiful, proud, vengeful. She came from a family almost overburdened with charismatic characters; generations of colourful men who had married formidable wives. Her grandfather was Duke William IX of Aquitaine and, as his Provençal *Vita* puts it, 'one of the most courtly men in the world, and one of the greatest deceivers of women.' In 1115 he fell seriously in love with Dangereuse, the wife of his vassal the Viscount of Châtellerault. Never a man to waste time, he carried off the Viscountess and installed her in a luxury apartment in the newly built Maubergeonne

ELEANOR
of
❧ AQUITAINE ❧

tower in his palace at Poitiers. Deeply offended, his wife Philippa withdrew herself decorously to the Abbey of Fontevrault, established in 1100 and already a favourite retreat for noble ladies, including William's rejected first wife Ermengarde. One of William's more prominent traits was that he didn't give a fig for the Church. He had already been excommunicated the previous year, but he was double-excommunicated for this scandalous flouting of law and morality. As it was out of the question for him ever to marry Dangereuse, they did the next best thing by marrying William's son William to Dangereuse's daughter Aenor in 1121. Eleanor was born the following year. One possible explanation of her name was that it derived from 'alia Aenor', the other Aenor. A sister, Petronilla, followed about eighteen months later - the two grew up in a close and loving relationship - and finally, a son and heir named (unsurprisingly) William.

The southern court in which Eleanor grew up was home to a leisured and cultured society; the famous troubadours Cercamon and Marcabru were both attached to this court for a time, along with a host of lesser stars. Eleanor acquired her great love of poetry and literature, fashion and sophistication, at an early age. She would have heard tales of King Arthur and the doomed love of Tristan and Isolde. She would also have drunk in the sparkling new ethos of 'courtly' love.

The troubadours combined the skills of poets, musicians, and singers; but they were much more than wandering minstrels. They were clever, sophisticated, witty, worldly, often highly educated. Their great subject was Love, and this was wildly novel. Love was to be desired as an end in itself; it inspired and ennobled the lover. The beloved woman was venerated as an object of worship; she was distant, aloof, usually superior in rank to the lover, and usually married; he was the supplicant, and if his prayers were denied, he suffered dreadful torments. This was revolutionary, because it placed women, who technically had no power, in a position of complete dominance over their lovers. For the first time in post-classical Europe a man's status as a member of courtly society was judged partly by his behaviour towards women. It cannot be over-emphasized how important this is when considering Eleanor. She adored troubadours, and always took some with her wherever she went.

Duke William IX died in 1127, when Eleanor was only five years old. He was a hard act to follow, and his son William X suffered by comparison. Though the chroniclers tellingly recorded him as a prickly tempered, stubborn, quarrelsome person, he too was a man of refined and sophisticated tastes and considerable education. These he passed on to his daughter. Unusually, Eleanor was taught to read, and carefully educated. She accompanied her parents on tours around their realms, receiving homage, hearing pleas, holding court, conducting business, quarrelling and being reconciled with unruly vassals.

A woodcut of The Romance of the Rose, *a poem which is the epitome of courtly love. Eleanor was very fond of poetry and was patron to a number of troubadours.*

In 1130 Eleanor's brother William died. His mother Aenor followed him a few months later. In 1136 William began to think about the precarious position of his family if he should die and leave a vulnerable young girl as his heir; he got himself betrothed to Emma, daughter and heiress of the Count of Limoges, and the widow of the Count of Cognac. But before he could actually marry her, she was abducted and married to Count William of Angoulême. He then made preparations to go on pilgrimage to the shrine of St James at Compostela in northern Spain. He left his daughters in the care of the Bishop of Bordeaux and in spring 1137 set off for Spain. On the way he was struck down by a wasting fever; he reached St James's Cathedral at Compostela only by being carried in on a litter, and died there on Easter Sunday. Before he died he confirmed Eleanor as the heiress of his vast dominions, and left her as the ward of his overlord, Louis VI 'the Fat' of France.

A musician accompanies a female singer who is reading from a manuscript – a fifteenth-century illustration to Vincent of Beauvais' Mirror of the World, *one of the first books printed in English by William Caxton.*

When news of William's death reached Louis in June, he himself was gravely ill, and lost no time in making arrangements to marry the fifteen-year-old Eleanor to his own sixteen-year-old son Louis, thus trebling the territories of the French Crown. It was too dangerous for Eleanor to make the journey through France, in case she should be seized and carried off by some nobleman looking to make his fortune. Instead the King despatched his son, accompanied by barons, knights, and troops and, after lavish celebrations and feasting, the marriage was celebrated on 25 July 1137. On 1 August Louis VI died. Suddenly Eleanor was Queen of France, as well as Duchess of Aquitaine.

Queen of France

Louis VII was the second son of his parents and had been brought up to enter the Church. He was a gentle, melancholy person, and extremely devout. The death of his elder brother Philippe had thrust him into prominence as the next heir and destined him for a very different, and probably uncongenial future.

One can only imagine how much of a shock all this was to Eleanor; within a matter of weeks, she had learned of her father's death, been married to the heir to the throne of France, then moved to the strange northern city of Paris as Queen. She brought to Paris her sister Petronilla and an entourage of fun-loving southern courtiers, and they settled into apartments in the royal palace on the Île de la Cité.

No chronicler reports that she felt homesick or confused, or irritated by her new husband, who practised religious austerities (Odo of Deuil described him as a man for whom 'worldly glory did not give sensual pleasure') but he was very different from the worldly, sophisticated, flattering men she was used to, and was probably something of a disappointment from the first. Several chroniclers agree that he was

ELEANOR
of
❧ AQUITAINE ❧

A glazed-terracotta statue of St Bernard, by the Della Robbia family in the abbey church of Santa Cruz in Florence, shows his qualities as a passionate reformer and powerful intellect.

besotted with Eleanor, and that she quickly gained a strong influence over him. It seems likely that Eleanor talked Louis into attempting to regain the county of Toulouse. She persuaded Louis to assert her rights by mounting a military campaign in the summer of 1141. The expedition was a dismal failure.

Eleanor's sister Petronilla, though only eighteen in 1141, had fallen in love with the ageing Count Raoul of Vermandois, who was in his fifties and already married to Leonore, a niece of Count Thibaut of Champagne. He had offended Louis by sheltering Pierre de la Châtre, whose appointment as an archbishop Louis had opposed. Raoul persuaded his brother, who was a bishop, and two other bishops, to prepare the usual excuse for ending an inconvenient marriage – that the couple were related to one another within the prohibited degree of kinship. But Count Thibaut was not prepared to accept this insult meekly. Clever and cautious, he had canon lawyers prepare a case against Raoul that the annulment had been made improperly and was not legally binding, and laid it before Pope Innocent. In June 1142 Innocent's legate in France held a council to investigate the case, and it declared that Raoul's marriage to Leonore was perfectly valid; Raoul himself, and Petronilla, and the three bishops who had obliged them in the matter of the annulment, were all excommunicated.

This was the last straw. Louis assembled his army, and invaded Champagne. In the Middle Ages the way to hurt an enemy was to attack and damage his lands, kill the innocent population, and pillage or destroy their possessions. Pitched battles, in which two armies confronted one another, were much rarer than these dreadful wars of attrition against poorly armed communities. Even for the time, Louis's army conducted itself with notorious ferocity and barbarity.

Louis pursued his vengeance with uncharacteristic determination, and despite a very stern letter from Bernard of Clairvaux which clearly hints where he thought the blame for Louis's actions lay:

From whom if not the devil has come this advice upon which you are acting, advice which has led to burnings upon burnings, slaughter upon slaughter...Those who are urging you to repeat your previous misdeeds against an innocent party [Thibaut] are not pursuing the cause of

your honour but of their own convenience, or rather the will of the devil; they are attempting to make use of your royal power in order to achieve insane goals which they could not hope to achieve by themselves; they are clearly the enemies of your crown and despoilers of your kingdom.

But Louis was unmoved. Not until 1144 was a peace negotiated by Abbot Suger and Abbot Bernard; Louis returned Champagne to Thibaut, and the interdict was lifted. Bernard is said to have prayed for an end to Eleanor's barrenness, and in 1145, after eight years of marriage to Louis, she gave birth to a daughter, Marie.

Eleanor the Crusader

The First Crusade in 1097-99 had been a great success and had enabled the combined forces of Christendom to carve out four Christian states from Muslim-held territory in the East. In terms of military strategy it was going to be impossibly difficult to hold onto them, but ideologically it seemed essential to do so. In December 1144 the Turkish Muslim forces of Nureddin recaptured the key city of Edessa on the north-eastern border of the crusader kingdom of Outremer. The following year the Latin princes of the crusader states appealed to the Pope for military aid to prevent Jerusalem falling into the hands of the Turks.

Louis announced his intention of taking the cross on Christmas Day, 1145. Months of preparation followed. On 31 March Louis actually 'took the cross': he accepted a mantle with a cross sewn onto it, from Bernard of Clairvaux's own hands. Eleanor, too, received the cross from St Bernard on that Easter Sunday. Louis

One of the sacred treasures that Eleanor might have seen in Constantinople or Jerusalem, if it hadn't been a fourteenth-century fake, the supposed veil of St Veronica bearing the miraculous image of Christ, better known to us as the Turin Shroud.

mobilized his army, and arranged with his fellow monarch, the Holy Roman Emperor Conrad, to meet his army at Constantinople.

Why did Eleanor go on crusade with her husband, leaving her two-year-old daughter behind in France? Pilgrimage meant penance, discomfort and hardship; but it also meant travel, the excitement of new places, exotic cultures, visits to hospitable foreign monarchs. Eleanor was by no means the only high-ranking lady to accompany her husband on this crusade. The chroniclers remarked what a nuisance it was to be burdened by their accommodations, servants, and baggage but Eleanor was a great feudal lord and, as she had recruited a great many of her own vassals from the south of France to go on the crusade, it was important for her to lead them in person.

So the army set forth with high hopes, enthusiasm for their cause, religious zeal, and excitement. They travelled through Bavaria and Hungary to Constantinople, reasonably without incident, but when they arrived at Constantinople, they found that Conrad had left without them, hurried on his way by Emperor Manuel Comnenus after his troops had disgraced themselves by their barbaric and undisciplined behaviour.

They pressed on towards Nicaea, where they encountered the worst of news. Conrad's army, a few days ahead of them, had been ambushed by the Turks at Dorylaeum, and virtually annihilated. Only a few hundred had survived out of about 10,000 men, and all Conrad's provisions, treasure, horses and weapons had been captured. He himself had escaped, but with serious head injuries. Louis and his council prepared to take the army across the mountains of Phrygia. Food was scarce, discipline virtually non-existent, and the soldiers had begun to sell their weapons and armour for food. To make matters worse, winter was coming on, with much worse weather than they had been led to expect. As they painfully wound across the tortuous and labyrinthine passes, they were constantly harassed and ambushed by the Turks; in January they came across the battleground of Dorylaeum, still littered with corpses. Ahead loomed Mount Cadmos. Louis took personal charge of the rear, which included the non-combatants and the baggage; the vanguard was commanded by Geoffrey de Rancon, one of Eleanor's Poitevin vassals. Geoffrey had been ordered to advance to the top of the mountain and make camp there, waiting for the slower rear to catch up; but for some reason he decided to advance a bit further to a nearby plateau. The army was strung out, the rear straggling, held back by the baggage. The Turks seized the top of the mountain and swarmed down on the unprepared Christians. Again, they managed to inflict a terrible defeat, almost massacring the panicking Franks. According to William of Tyre, 'our people were hindered by the narrow paths, and their horses exhausted by the great weight of the baggage.' Much of this baggage and valuable equipment was lost. Louis barely escaped with his life, his bodyguard slaughtered around him.

Though the fiasco of the crossing of Mount Cadmos exposed Louis's inadequacies as a military leader, it was – most unfairly – Eleanor who was blamed for it. More than one chronicler reported that the baggage so disastrously separated from the main army consisted of Eleanor's and her companions' clothes and other useless encumbrances. Louis decided to make for Antioch and the civilized court of Prince Raymond, where they might hope to win some time to recover strength before pushing on. The rest of the journey was a nightmare, according to Odo of Deuil and William of Tyre. The crusaders had lost their provisions and had little food and no water. They bled their horses to drink their blood, and ate the flesh of horses and asses killed in the fighting. When they arrived they were impoverished, dressed in rags, many shoeless, starving and sick.

Antioch must have seemed paradisal by comparison. But, though Antioch could still furnish luxuries and banquets, Raymond knew himself to be in a precarious position and he needed the crusaders' help. After Edessa, Antioch was obviously Nureddin's next target, and then nothing would prevent the Turks from sweeping down to recover Jerusalem. It would be in the interests of the whole of the Eastern Christian kingdom, Raymond argued, for the crusaders to turn aside for a while and help him to make a decisive strike against the Turks in the north by attacking Nureddin's city of Aleppo, and strengthen his position for the future.

John of Salisbury reports that during the ten days Eleanor spent in Antioch she and Prince Raymond were frequently together and engaged in 'constant, almost continuous conversations', which aroused the worst suspicions and passionate jealousy in Louis. Raymond was by all accounts everything Louis was not – tall, handsome, vigorous, decisive, masculine. He was also her father's youngest brother, though only eight years older than Eleanor herself. Whether one believes the scurrilous hints of several chroniclers that Eleanor actually did commit adultery (and incest) with Raymond or not, it is clear that Louis, possibly egged on by his closest companions, believed there was more to the hours of constant conversation than a recital of Raymond's hopes and plans for military aid. These plans made sense to Eleanor, but if Raymond hoped that by his attentions to her he would recommend himself and his proposals to Louis, or that she would influence Louis in his favour, he was to be disappointed. Louis

ELEANOR of ❦ AQUITAINE ❦

A stereotyped description of a battle in early sixteenth-century dress and armour, this nonetheless gives an idea of the sights that confronted Eleanor during the disastrous Second Crusade.

ELEANOR
of
❦ AQUITAINE ❦.

A beautiful illustration in the Chroniques de St. Denis *showing Louis VII and his ally on the Second Crusade, the Holy Roman Emperor Conrad III, entering Constantinople together. In fact this never happened – Conrad and his German army had already left by the time Louis and Eleanor arrived.*

flatly refused. He made preparations to leave for Jerusalem within days of his arrival. He clearly had the support of his principal commanders in this. To the Franks, the Aquitainian Raymond was equally a foreigner, who planned to borrow their military support merely in order to enlarge his own territories, and this had nothing to do with the original objectives of the crusade. This story is taken up by John of Salisbury in his Historia Pontificalis:

> *And when the king made haste to tear [the queen] away, she mentioned their kinship, saying it was not lawful for them to remain together as man and wife, since they were related ... At this the king was most deeply moved; and although he loved the queen almost beyond reason he consented to divorce her if his councellors and the French nobility would allow it. There was one knight among the king's secretaries, called Thierry Galeran ... whom the queen had always hated and mocked, but who was faithful... He boldly persuaded the king not to suffer her to dally longer at Antioch, ... because it would be a lasting shame to the kingdom of the Franks if in addition to all the other disasters it was reported that the king had been deserted by his wife, or robbed of her. So he argued, either because he hated the queen or because he really believed it, moved perchance by widespread rumour. In consequence, she was torn away and forced to leave for Jerusalem with the king; and, their mutual anger growing greater, the wound remained, hide it as best they might.*

We can only imagine how Eleanor fumed as she was forced to accompany Louis to Jerusalem. In June a council of war was convened at Acre, where the newly recovered Emperor Conrad had appeared with the remnants of his army. Since the crusaders had rejected Raymond of Antioch's sensible plan, and since Jerusalem was not in any immediate danger of attack, a catastrophically stupid decision was taken to attack the Muslim state of Damascus. Damascus was just about the only Muslim state willing to be on good terms with the Christians, because the emir had quarrelled with Nureddin. Now, however, as the crusader army settled down around his city walls, he was obliged to beg Nureddin for help and supplies. But the crusaders were there for less than a week; on 28 July, Louis ordered the army to retreat to Jerusalem, having heard that Nureddin had arrived with reinforcements. The Turks poured out of Damascus to slaughter the panicking Christians, and inflicted a savage humiliation, and the final one; losses of men and equipment were so great that there was nothing for it but to return to France.

Eleanor is not mentioned in the accounts of this period or the subsequent one of several months while Louis hung about in Jerusalem, putting off his return to France, but we can be sure that the wounds in their marriage did not heal. When they eventually returned, in spring 1149, it was in separate ships.

Eleanor was by now thoroughly disillusioned with her husband, and wanted to be rid of him. William of Newburgh recorded her celebrated remark that 'she had married a monk, not a king'; and judging by the evidence of Eleanor's glorious fertility during her second marriage, this was a complaint about a man with a very low sex drive from a woman with a very high one. The couple visited Pope Eugenius who interviewed the two separately. He listened to their doubts on the issue of consanguinity – that they were so closely related that their union had displeased God, as was patently evident since in twelve years of marriage they had only managed to produce one daughter. But Eugenius confirmed the legality of their union, and according to John of Salisbury, 'he ordered that no one should speak a word against it, and that it must not be dissolved under any pretext whatever, on pain of anathema.' He then personally escorted them to a bed he had had specially prepared. While this may not have been a successful method of restoring the marriage, Eleanor became pregnant soon afterwards. But, fortunately for her, she gave birth to another girl, useless for dynastic purposes, and this was the decisive factor in gaining her freedom from her hated marriage. Louis was now badgered by his barons to get rid of Eleanor; he must marry again and beget sons.

Queen of England

In August 1151 Geoffrey Plantagenet, 'the handsome' Count of Anjou, visited the court of King Louis with his teenaged son Henry to negotiate a truce in hostilities between them. Geoffrey was married to the Empress Matilda, rightful heir to the throne of England and the duchy of Normandy. While she struggled to regain the throne of England from the usurping King Stephen, Geoffrey had seized

ELEANOR
of
❦ AQUITAINE ❦

Normandy in 1144, and in 1150 made it over to his son. This fief was held from the King of France, but Henry had not so far done homage to Louis for it.

Geoffrey and his son were impressive figures - handsome, vigorous, energetic, decisive. Eleanor knew that the annulment of her marriage was inevitable and would not be long in coming, and must have been thinking about what she would do with herself and her huge dominions afterwards. There is no record of a meeting between the Plantagenets and Eleanor during that August, but William of Newburgh, writing with hindsight in the 1190s, stated that '... she resolved to marry the Duke of Normandy ... and for this reason she desired and brought about the divorce'. Gerald of Wales, a writer with no fondness for Eleanor or Henry, gleefully recorded a scurrilous rumour about her:

> Geoffrey, count of Anjou, had seduced Queen Eleanor when he was seneschal of France; on account of which, it is said, he often warned his son Henry, advising and forbidding him to touch her in any way, both because she was the wife of his lord, and because she had been known carnally by his own father.

But, given the swiftness with which the marriage took place after Eleanor's liberation, it must have been plotted beforehand, and this is when it must have been done. Although Eleanor was twenty-nine years old, and Henry only eighteen and, although they must have known that their union would enrage Louis and his supporters, there were clear advantages to both of them in the match. Henry, as the son of Matilda, had a serious and legitimate claim to the throne of England; but even without it, his French domains united with Eleanor's would create a power base much greater than the King's. We have no reliable record of Eleanor's appearance, but all the chroniclers say that she was beautiful. She was vastly wealthy. She was also, after years of a loveless marriage to a man who clearly did not perform his conjugal obligations very often, in her sexual prime. Henry had plenty of excitingly masculine qualities: no one would mistake him for a monk.

The formal proceedings for the annulment were held on 21 March 1152 at Beaugency. Witnesses testified that the King and Queen were related within the prohibited degrees of kinship. Custody of the two little princesses, now aged seven and three, was awarded to their father. Eleanor was permitted to retain her dominions, and to remarry, provided that she continued to do homage to Louis as her overlord. The proceedings concluded, Eleanor and her retinue left for Poitiers. A measure of how important it was for Eleanor to marry again quickly is that not one but two attempts were made by opportunistic younger sons to abduct her on this journey; one by Thibaut of Blois, and one by Henry's own younger brother Geoffrey. She successfully evaded both, and was back home by Easter, gleefully cancelling every piece of legislation she had enacted with Louis. She was also conducting secret negotiations with Henry Plantagenet – so secret that no trace of them remains. Eleanor was flouting feudal law, which required that as Louis's vassal and ward she should obtain his consent before marrying. Henry arrived at Poitiers in mid-May, and they were married on the 18th, not eight weeks since her annulment. Cheekily, Eleanor arranged for experts in canon law to issue legal dispensations for the marriage to take place, for she was even more closely related to Henry than she had been to Louis.

Louis responded by combining his forces with those of several other powerful nobles who had scores to settle with Henry Plantagenet (including King Stephen and Henry's own younger brother Geoffrey), and invaded Normandy. But Henry, an able military commander, swiftly disposed of the threat by marching past them and counter-attacking in their own territories, dividing and conquering.

Henry, though a strong contender for the throne of England through the claim of his mother Matilda, was not the only candidate. King Stephen had a son, Eustace; Louis now arranged a marriage between Eustace and his sister, supporting and validating Eustace's claim to the throne in no uncertain terms.

Eleanor began a major tour of her domains in the south, reasserting her authority over her vassals by receiving homage, confirming existing privileges, granting new ones. She had a new seal made, which survives on various charters she made at this time, in which she grandly reiterates all her titles : 'Eleanor, by the grace of God, duchess of Aquitaine and Normandy, countess of Anjou, Poitou, and Maine.' These charters are in Eleanor's name, but they mention her as 'united with the Duke of Normandy and Count of Anjou ... my very noble lord Henry' — she was clearly proud of her new alliance. In August Henry joined her on her tour and the couple spent four months together. In January 1153, Henry left his mother in charge of Normandy, and Eleanor, now pregnant, in charge of Anjou and Maine as well as her own territories. He crossed the Channel with a small army. His successful siege of Malmesbury Castle was followed by a confrontation close to Wallingford; Stephen and Henry had begun to talk peace when news arrived which transformed their negotiations. As chronicler Henry of Huntingdon wrote:

> *As usual, God was on the side of the duke ... light had begun to dawn on the great duke's fortunes. For two of his most powerful and hostile enemies, namely the king's son Eustace and Simon, Earl of Northampton, were snatched away together by the providence of God, and as a result all who opposed the duke lost courage and despaired ... By removing the most dangerous adversaries of his beloved Henry, God was most kindly preparing the way for his peaceful reign.*

Crushed, King Stephen met Henry at Winchester and agreed to adopt him as his heir. They confirmed a peace treaty, according to which Stephen was to rule for the rest of his life, and Henry was to inherit the kingdom after his death. From Winchester they travelled to London, and from there to Oxford; on this progress

ELEANOR of ❦ AQUITAINE ❦

The seal of Louis VII of France. The side shown in the top picture bears the title 'Dux Aquitanorum', meaning that he was Eleanor's husband. Eleanor was an exceptioanlly powerful woman in an age where women usually played a submissive role.

47

all the chief nobles of England did homage and promised fealty to Henry as their next king. After almost twenty years of bitter and damaging civil war, the joy of the people and the enthusiasm of the magnates reported by the chroniclers as standard on such occasions was certainly genuine this time. And Henry had another reason to celebrate; within a week of the death of Prince Eustace, Eleanor had a son, whom she named William. Henry returned to Normandy, to his mother's court at Rouen, in spring 1154; Eleanor joined him in June and, following what would become an established pattern in their marriage, quickly became pregnant again. In October King Stephen died, aged fifty-eight. Henry and Eleanor were crowned King and Queen of England at Westminster Abbey on 19 December.

Eleanor gave birth to a second son at the end of February, 1155; he was named Henry. Henry himself was working like a demon to restore order to a country whose institutions and economy had been seriously damaged by the long years of civil war. Eleanor often accompanied her husband on his exhausting tours around his new kingdom. She had her own income from her own territories and, judging by the surviving records of her household expenditure, she enjoyed a luxurious lifestyle, attracting criticism and disapproval from John of Salisbury in *Policraticus* and Walter Map, whose delightfully gossipy *De Nugis Curialum* (*Courtiers'*

The exquisitely enamelled tomb effigy in Le Mans Cathedral of Geoffery 'the Handsome' Plantagenet, Count of Anjou, Duke of Normandy; rumoured to have been Eleanor's lover, and the father of her second husband, Henry II of England.

Trifles) contains anecdotes about the leisure activities of the court. The King and Queen were passionately fond of hunting; both enjoyed the daring new polyphonic music; a constant stream of foreign visitors kept them abreast of the latest developments in literature, culture, fashion; and, as always, Eleanor had musicians, poets, minstrels, creating a milieu of sophisticated entertainment.

Eleanor participated actively in the business of government, often acting as her husband's deputy in England when he spent months touring his domains in France. She seems to have enjoyed Henry's full confidence, not unreasonably, as she had many more years experience of statecraft. During the first eleven or twelve years of their marriage, though they did not spend much time together, they met up regularly once or twice a year, at Christmas and Easter, and these meetings were extraordinarily fruitful. After the birth of little Prince Henry in February 1155, Eleanor then gave birth to Matilda in the summer of 1156, Richard in September

1157, Geoffrey in September 1158, Eleanor in 1161, Joanna in 1165, and finally John on Christmas Eve, 1166, when Eleanor herself was forty-four years old. But by this time, Eleanor was well aware that the virile Henry was quite astoundingly unfaithful, producing illegitimate children here, there, and everywhere, including one who, according to Walter Map, was the son of a common prostitute called Ykenai, who 'stooped to all uncleanness'. Henry acknowledged this son, born not long after Prince William, as his own and named him Geoffrey. Later, somewhat unconventionally, he was brought into the royal household and Eleanor was put in charge of his upbringing! She seems to have been fond of the boy, who was destined for a splendid career in the church. Perhaps he reminded her of William, who had sadly died at the age of only three in 1156.

Besides his infidelity, however, Henry was a very stubborn and determined character who was not as susceptible to her influence as the vacillating Louis had been. Irritatingly, Henry was completely infatuated with Thomas Becket. Henry heaped riches and honours on his friend and companion, while his wife became increasingly estranged. Becket had also been Prince Henry's tutor since the little boy was five years old. But in 1162, Becket was elected Archbishop of Canterbury, and his relationship with Henry rapidly deteriorated. Suddenly Becket was no longer the king's loyal friend and right-hand man, but the champion of the Church and a formidable opponent. Henry's astonishment soon turned to fury when he found that his former friend refused to support his decisions, and their dispute escalated over the following eight years, culminating in Becket's murder in 1170. There's a strong historical tradition that Eleanor disliked Becket and encouraged Henry to quarrel with him and to feel bitter and resentful towards him (which he certainly did).

In the late 1160s Eleanor spent increasing amounts of time in her French territories. Prince Henry was crowned as Henry the Young King in 1170. At the same time Eleanor had the young Prince Richard confirmed as Duke of Aquitaine at Poitiers, where she now settled with her court.

Patron of the Arts

Both Eleanor and Henry were very actively involved with the latest trends in secular literature. Traditionally poets could find wealthy patrons not only by composing works in their honour but also

Paintings of the tomb effigies of Henry and Eleanor at the Abbey of Fontevrault. No trace now remains of the original paint.

ELEANOR
of
❦ AQUITAINE ❧

by dedicating works to them. The royal couple must have encouraged the production of the brand new kind of literature, the romance – the three earliest surviving romances, *Le Roman d'Eneas*, *Le Roman de Thèbes*, and *Le Roman de Troie* by Benoît de Sainte-Maure, were all composed during their reigns, and in their territory. Benoît includes a compliment to Eleanor in the prologue to the *Roman de Troie*, calling her the '*riche dame de riche rei*'.

A vogue for Arthurian literature was begun by Geoffrey of Monmouth, who completed his epic *Historia regum Britanniae* (*History of the Kings of Britain*) in 1136. In 1155 Geoffrey's 'history' was translated into Anglo-Norman French by a man named Wace, and then into English (still very close to Anglo-Saxon). Wace presented a copy of his translation to Eleanor. Henry liked Wace's work so much that he commissioned him to write a history of the Dukes of Normandy. A celebrated woman poet, Marie de France, also frequented the English royal court, and dedicated her short verse Breton *lais* – love stories featuring knights and ladies, often with a strong supernatural element – to Henry.

Eleanor was herself the subject of flattering verses, some of which refer to her very openly, like this wistful anonymous German lyric:

> *If all the world were mine*
> *From sea shore to the Rhine,*
> *That price were not too high,*
> *To have England's queen lie*
> *Close in my arms.*

A drawing of one of Eleanor's seals, showing a slender, elegantly dressed queen and bearing her chief titles: Queen of the English and Duchess of the Normans. It also gives the medieval form of her name, Aliénor.

There is a series of poems by the famous troubadour Bernard de Ventadour, in which the poet expresses his hopeless passion for his mistress, who is far above him in rank, without naming her. Bernard's biographer was less discreet:

> *He went to the Duchess of Normandy, who was young and of great worth,*
> *and had great understanding of merit, honour, and songs of praise.*
> *Bernard's poems and songs pleased her greatly, and she made him warmly*
> *welcome. He stayed at her court for a long time, and fell in love with her,*
> *and so did she with him; and he composed many wonderful songs for her.*
> *While they were together, King Henry of England took her as his wife and*
> *brought her from Normandy to England. Bernard stayed behind, full of*
> *grief and sorrow, and then he went to the good Count Raymond of*
> *Toulouse, with whom he remained until his death.*

There are obvious historical innacuracies here, not least that Eleanor was not the Duchess of Normandy until Henry married her, but we know that she had Bernard with her at Angers all the time she was acting as regent for Henry in 1153. She was pregnant that year with her eldest son William, and perhaps it was that which made it safe for her to enjoy a dalliance with the gifted Bernard; we certainly shouldn't assume that Eleanor's reputation for adultery was completely unfounded. Here is part of one of Bernard's poems in which he laments the loss of his lady:

> *Alas, I thought I knew so much*
> *Of love, and yet I know so little!*
> *For I cannot stop myself loving her*
> *From whom I shall never have joy.*
> *My whole heart, and all of me from myself*
> *She has taken, and her own self, and all the world,*
> *For when she took herself from me, she left me nothing*
> *But desire and a yearning heart.*

Another writer connects Eleanor explicitly with the cult of Fin Amors, whose principal characteristic is that it is incompatible with marriage. This was Andreas Capellanus, who claims to have been a chaplain in a royal household. Andreas was writing probably between 1184 and 1186, by which time the ethos of courtly love was fully explored and codified. Andreas wrote a long Latin treatise called *De arte honesti amandi* (*On the Art of Honourable Loving*). Andreas often mentions Eleanor's eldest daughter and, since it is known that she had a chaplain called André, it is often assumed that he worked for her. Medieval people were extremely fond of codes and rules and lists of things; much medieval literature consists of treatises and guides on chivalry, hunting, table manners; it is only surprising that this is the only one on correct behaviour for lovers. Andreas, tongue-in-cheek, presents us with a vision of a courtly society in which people enjoyed debating the various rights and wrongs of romantic love in mock 'court-cases', which were presided over by great ladies. Two of these ladies were Marie de Champagne and Eleanor herself. Here, Andreas quotes Marie as giving a definitive decision about the propriety of love within marriage:

> *We state and consider as firmly established, that love cannot exert its powers between two married people. For lovers give everything to one another freely, not by reason of force or necessity. Married people, on the other hand, have to obey each other's wishes out of duty, and can deny nothing of themselves to one another. Besides, how does it increase a husband's honour, if he enjoys his wife's embraces like a lover, since neither one of them will be improved in worth or virtue by this, and they seem to possess nothing but what they have always had a right to? And we shall assert yet another reason: for a precept of love informs us, that no woman, even a married woman, can be crowned with the prize of the King of Love unless she is perceived to be enlisted in love's service outside the bonds of matrimony. And indeed another rule of love teaches that no one can be wounded by love for two men. Therefore, Love cannot rightly acknowledge that he has any rights between married people.*

ELEANOR
of
❦ AQUITAINE ❦

Andreas seems to have intended this sort of thing as an elaborate literary joke. He follows up this absurd declaration with some examples of case histories submitted for judgement; this is the one he ascribes to Queen Eleanor:

> *A certain knight was bound by love to a woman who was tied to the love of another man, but from her he got this much hope of her love: that, if at some time she happened to be deprived of the love of her lover, then she would grant her love to this knight. A short time later, this woman and her lover were married. The knight then demanded to be shown the fruition of the hope she had given him; the woman however absolutely refused, saying that she had not lost her beloved's love. In this case, the Queen responded as follows: 'We do not dare to set ourselves against the opinion of the Countess of Champagne, who set down as her judgement that love cannot exert any power between husband and wife. Therefore we recommend that the lady should make good her promise of love.'*

Thomas Becket, Archbishop of Canterbury, takes his leave with what looks like a rather rude gesture at Kings Henry II and Louis VII after a failed attempt at reconciliation: an illustration from a Medieval Life of the Martyred Saint, *c.1235.*

If these really are the words of Marie and Eleanor – and surely Andreas would scarcely dare to write the attribution if they were not – then we see the pair of them participating in an elaborate intellectual game, in which each of them tries desperately to outdo the other in carrying the 'precepts' of courtly love to ridiculous extremes. Marie's denunciation of married love is so forthright and so over-emphatic, that the coolly ironic tone of Eleanor's rejoinder is exquisitely witty – as if one could imagine such a formidable woman as Eleanor being frightened to disagree with her daughter.

Despite the fact that Eleanor had seen very little of her since the divorce from Louis when she was seven years old, Marie seems to have got on well with her mother at this time of her life, some twenty-five years later. A strong historical tradition has her paying extended visits to Eleanor's court at Poitiers during the 1170s, when Eleanor certainly was there administering the Duchy of Aquitaine on behalf of the adolescent Richard. Growing up in such a richly endowed cultural environment, Richard also wrote troubadour lyrics of hopeless devotion.

A medieval illustration of the crowning of a King. Young Henry was given the title of king but was allowed little real power by his father.

Power-broker, Conspirator, Political Prisoner

In 1170 Eleanor, though no longer as close to Henry as she had been, was still prepared to take his part in the Becket debate. For example, Henry arranged to have his eldest son Henry crowned (as Henry the Young King) by the Archbishop of York, instead of by Becket, whose prerogative as Archbishop of Canterbury it was. The Pope sent the Bishop of Worcester with a formal notice forbidding him to do this, but Henry travelled to England with the boy while Eleanor detained the bishop at Caen, so that the Pope's letter could not reach him in time.

The young Henry, was already feeling angry and restless; he now had the name of king, but his father allowed him no real executive power. A change was also becoming apparent in Eleanor; she no longer automatically identified with her husband's interests, but took the part of her sons, even when they opposed him. In 1173 the young Henry quarrelled with his father, who forced him, more or less under house arrest, to accompany him north to Normandy; at Chinon where they had made an overnight stop, the young Henry somehow managed to escape from the castle and fled south again to Eleanor at Poitou. There he plotted with his brothers Richard and Geoffrey, and, according to William of Newburgh, Eleanor.

Henry ordered Eleanor and his sons to join him; she ignored him and all three sons went off together to Paris, to the court of Henry's arch-enemy Louis. The results of their conspiracy were beginning to be apparent in several open rebellions by discontented barons. Eleanor had initially stayed behind at Poitou, but Henry was marching south with his armies of mercenaries. According to Gervase of Canterbury, she set off for Paris with a small retinue of knights, and disguised herself in men's clothing. The disguise was not enough; on the way she fell into the hands of someone (we don't know who) still loyal to her husband, was captured, and handed over to Henry. He was so furious at her disloyalty – and so perturbed by her influence over the boys – that he kept her a virtual prisoner for the next sixteen years. He descended on Poitiers and disbanded her court. In the course of the following year Henry met with his three rebellious sons to make peace terms. They had to promise never to 'demand anything further from the Lord King, their father, beyond the agreed settlement ... and withdraw neither themselves nor their service from him.' They were then reconciled to the paternal bosom. But there was no forgiveness for Eleanor, under house arrest, probably at Salisbury Castle.

Records of the Queen's activities are almost non-existent for the next ten years. Her household was very small; she did not receive guests or give hospitality. A poem composed by one Richard le Poitevin records a moving lament for Eleanor's straitened circumstances:

> *Tell me, Eagle with two heads, tell me: where were you when your eaglets, flying from their nest, dared to raise their talons against the king of the North Wind? It was you, we learn, who urged them to rise against their father. That is why you have been plucked from your own country and carried away to an alien land. ... Eagle of the broken alliance, how much longer will you cry out unanswered? The king of the North Wind holds you in captivity. But do not despair: lift your voice like a bugle and it shall reach the ears of your sons. The day will come when they will set you free and you shall come again to dwell in your native land.*

In 1183 Henry the Young King was again quarrelling with his father. Much to the scandal of the chroniclers, when the elder Henry cut off his allowance, he took to plundering like any brigand, and in June he plundered the shrine of Rocamadour. Divine retribution for this sacrilegious act was not long in coming; within hours the young king had been struck down by the 'flux of the bowels' (probably dysentery) and it soon became clear that he would not recover. He sent his father a message asking him to have mercy on Eleanor, then laid himself on a bed of ashes in token of penitence, and died on 11 June, aged only twenty-eight.

Henry was buried in Rouen Cathedral. Eleanor was not allowed to attend; but after this her confinement was less restricted, so it seems that Henry was moved by the dying wish of his son. In 1184 we learn of Eleanor crossing to France on Henry's orders to make a tour of her 'dower' lands. That Christmas she spent at Windsor with Richard and John – the first time she had been allowed to see them for ten years – and Matilda and her children. She also saw her second surviving son, Geoffrey, now Count of Brittany, at Westminster; and this was for the last time – the following August he was killed at a tournament in Paris.

Relations between parents and sons now polarized; Henry favoured John, Eleanor Richard. John had been made King of Ireland; Richard had asked his father to confirm him as his heir, and Henry had refused, leading to suspicions that Henry might disinherit him in favour of John. To add insult to injury, Henry had

A wallpainting of Eleanor found in a chapel in Chinon. Eleanor was immensely famous in her own lifetime, and images of her were found throughout Europe.

taken the Princess Alice, sister of Margaret and half-sister of the new young king of France, Philip, as his mistress, even though she was supposedly betrothed to Richard. Richard formed a very close relationship with Philip, even, it was rumoured, sharing his bed. He also took the cross, and promised himself in a new crusade to recover Jerusalem, recently reconquered by Saladin. In 1189 Philip and Richard combined their forces to attack Henry's cities of Le Mans and Tours, and Henry, now sick with an ulcerated wound, was compelled to accept their peace terms. He had stipulated that they should provide him with a list of those who had originally supported him but had changed sides, though he promised not to pursue vengeance against them. When this list was brought to him, it was headed by his favourite son, John. This was the final blow; Henry became delirious, and died the following day. His body was carried to the Abbey of Fontevrault for burial.

Queen Mother

Eleanor was now sixty-seven years old but was still ready for action. Richard remained in France, took his place as Duke of Normandy, and made an agreement to go on crusade with the King the following year. Eleanor toured England making sure of the barons' support for her son, putting into effect a general amnesty of prisoners, and organizing the coronation, which took place in early September.

Richard did not plan to remain in England very long; he had spent his formative years in France and doesn't seem to have cared much for England except as a source of revenue. He was planning, with the meticulous forethought and practical energy of an excellent general, raising and provisioning and paying and transporting a huge army to the Holy Land for his crusade. He set off in July for

ELEANOR
of
❧ AQUITAINE ❧

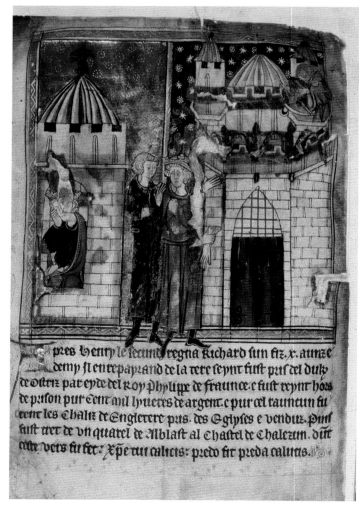

Italy, planning to meet up with Philip Augustus in Sicily. Eleanor, meanwhile, had decided that he should marry the Princess Berengaria, daughter of King Sancho of Navarre. He was officially still betrothed to Alice, the half-sister of Philip Augustus, who, when he heard of Eleanor's plan, insisted that Richard honour his engagemen. Richard refused, on the grounds that she had been his father's mistress, and had born him a son. Philip was obliged to accept this and Eleanor and Berengaria arrived to join Richard in Sicily. Berengaria travelled on to Cyprus with Richard, where he married her and had her crowned Queen of England.

Philip Augustus did not stay long on crusade; after the successful siege of Acre in July 1192 he fell ill and, returned to France, his relationship with Richard having turned sour. Richard also fell ill and, after being advised that there would be no point in recapturing Jerusalem as the Christians would not be able to hold onto it, he decided to return home. On the way he was shipwrecked, taken captive by Duke Leopold of Austina placed him in the castle of Durrenstein and informed his cousin the Holy Roman Emperor of his catch. The ransom was 100,000 marks of silver plus, 200 hostages from the families of his vassals. Richard was transferred to the Emperor Henry's castle at Hagenau, from where he wrote furious letters to the emperor, to his vassals, to his mother, and poems expressing the anguish he felt. One of these was to his half-sister Marie de Champagne:

A prisoner must truthfully express his feelings of bitter grief, but he can still console himself by composing a song. I have many friends, but their gifts are mean, which will be a shame to them if, for want of the ransom, I have to stay here as a prisoner for two winters. My barons and vassals, of England, Normandy, Poitou and Gascony, know well that I would never leave one of my friends to rot in prison for want of money. I do not say this to reproach them, but I myself am still a prisoner.

Richard's territories had already been severely taxed to raise money for his crusade, and the task of extracting this new levy from the impoverished people of England and Normandy fell to Eleanor. John made his sympathies clear by having himself proclaimed Richard's heir and going to France, where he made an agreement with Philip Augustus – Philip accepted John's homage for the Plantagenet territories in France and would support him as the next king of England, in return for John ceding the disputed territory of the Vexin to the French Crown. Eleanor responded to by closing the Channel ports and putting England in a state of defence. She spent most of 1193 working to collect the ransom money. Eleanor also had to persuade nobles of the rank of baron and above to part with 200 hostages from their families. All this accomplished, she set off in December with the money (thirty-five tons of silver!), the hostages, and her retinue. She arrived ready to complete the release of her son, to find that John had concocted a new scheme with Philip Augustus, namely that they should offer Emperor Henry the same amount of silver to keep Richard imprisoned for a further nine months. Fortunately for Richard, Emperor Henry was persuaded by his vassals to release Richard to his mother. After a triumphant tour round England and his French territories, and a new coronation, Richard was reconciled with John, apparently through Eleanor's persuasion, on the grounds that it was better to be on good terms with him than drive him to further deceit and treachery with Philip.

However, the stresses of this experience came back upon Eleanor when it was over, and in 1194 she retired temporarily to her favourite Abbey of Fontevrault. Here she remained in peace and quiet for five years, occasionally lending her influence when requested in the affairs of this or that abbey or vassal. In 1199 Richard was besieging the fortress of Châlus, almost as a recreation – it was small and poorly armed. As the King was walking the rounds in the early evening on 25 March, he was struck in the shoulder by an arrow. After some brutish and inept surgery, the wound turned gangrenous and it became clear that he would die. He sent for Eleanor; she hurried the 100 miles from Fontevrault to be by his side and he died in her arms on 6 April.

Richard had named John as heir. But between Richard and John there had been Geoffrey; and Geoffrey had left a son, Arthur, the twelve-year-old count of Brittany. His mother Constance had been regent on his behalf and now asserted his claim to the throne of England and duchy of Normandy, supported in the latest twist of the Plantagenet plot,

ELEANOR
of
❧ AQUITAINE ❧.

A richly coloured manuscript illustration of the Kings of England. Pictured are Henry II, Richard I, John and Henry III.

ELEANOR
of
❧ AQUITAINE ❧

by the scheming Philip Augustus. Many barons were deeply unimpressed by John, and a whole wedge of them in Anjou, Maine, and Touraine, declared themselves for Arthur. Arthur did homage to Philip for these counties, and joined forces with Philip to seize control of Angers and Le Mans (capitals of Anjou and Maine). Immediately Eleanor, who had been staying at Fontevrault since Richard's funeral there, took control of Richard's mercenary forces under their captain Mercadier and, despite her seventy-seven years, marched with them to recover Angers. John on his part showed energy and efficiency in recapturing Le Mans. Eleanor consolidated John's position in Anjou and Maine while he took himself off to be crowned at Westminster; then after another brief rest at Fontevrault she embarked on an exhausting political tour of Aquitaine to assert her rights as duchess.

By early 1200 Philip Augustus and John had agreed a treaty by which Philip accepted John as Richard's heir and Arthur's feudal lord. They also agreed to marry Eleanor's grand-daughter Blanche of Castile to Philip's son and heir Louis. Eleanor set off on the arduous journey to Spain to fetch the child-bride. Her mission safely accomplished, she withdrew again to Fontevrault, leaving the Archbishop of Bordeaux to escort Blanche to Normandy for her wedding.

But, although Eleanor had been supremely successful in her attempts to hold the Plantagenet empire together, it was a very large thorn in the side of the French king and his ultimate aim was to seize back as much of it as he could. In 1202 Philip found a pretext for dispossessing John of his French territories and, disregarding the peace treaty, he attacked Normandy, once more in alliance with Arthur of Brittany. He then marched on Poitiers. This outrageous attack catapulted Eleanor out of retirement once more, but she made her way towards Poitiers slowly, probably because of poor health. While she was staying at the castle of Mirebeau,

Eleanor's tomb effigy at Fontevrault. She lies between Henry II of England and Richard.

her grandson Arthur attacked and besieged it. Eleanor sent a messenger riding off to John at Le Mans. Mirebeau could not hold out long, as it was not provisioned to withstand a siege, and it wasn't long before eighty year old Eleanor and her small force was beleaguered in the keep, playing for time by negotiating. According to the unknown author of the *Histoire des ducs de Normandie*:

> *Arthur contrived to parley with his grandmother, demanding that she surrender the castle and make over all her possessions to him. She could then go in peace wherever she wished, for he had no wish to show her anything but honour. The queen replied that she would not leave, and that he should leave the place at once ... for he could easily find many other castles to attack than the one she was in.*

Eleanor's response shows her courage and style. Knowing that her supplies were low and, trusting to John's habitual late and inept military activity, Arthur felt secure. Le Mans was eighty miles away from Mirebeau; but to everyone's surprise, John had made a forced march to come to his mother's rescue and covered it in two days. The gates had been left open, and he attacked at dawn, before they could be closed. He achieved a great coup – as he put it in a letter to his English vassals:

> *God's grace has been bountiful to us ... when we were on route to Chinon, we learned that our lady mother was closely besieged at Mirebeau and we hastened there as fast as we could. And there we took captive our nephew Arthur, Geoffrey de Lusignan, Hugh le Brun [de Lusignan], Andre de Chauvigny, the Viscount of Chatellerault, Raymond Thouars, Savary de Mauleon, Hugh Bauge, and all our other Poitevin enemies who were present, almost two hundred knights, and not one of them escaped. God be praised for our victory.*

It was indeed a triumph; for this roll-call included almost all the rebels who had been assisting Arthur against him and, more importantly, Arthur was now in his power. Eleanor had braved a crisis, but would pay the penalty in health afterwards. She retired to Fontevrault and was unable to help as John, instead of consolidating his gains, alienated his allies and began to lose portions of his great inheritance to Philip Augustus (but not to Arthur, who disappeared into the dungeons of Falaise and was never seen again). In March 1204 John's tardiness and ineffectualness lost him Richard I's castle of Château Gaillard, the strategically crucial point from which Philip would subsequently be able to conquer Normandy. By this time Eleanor was overwhelmed by a deep sleep from which she would never awaken. She died peacefully on 1 April, 1204.

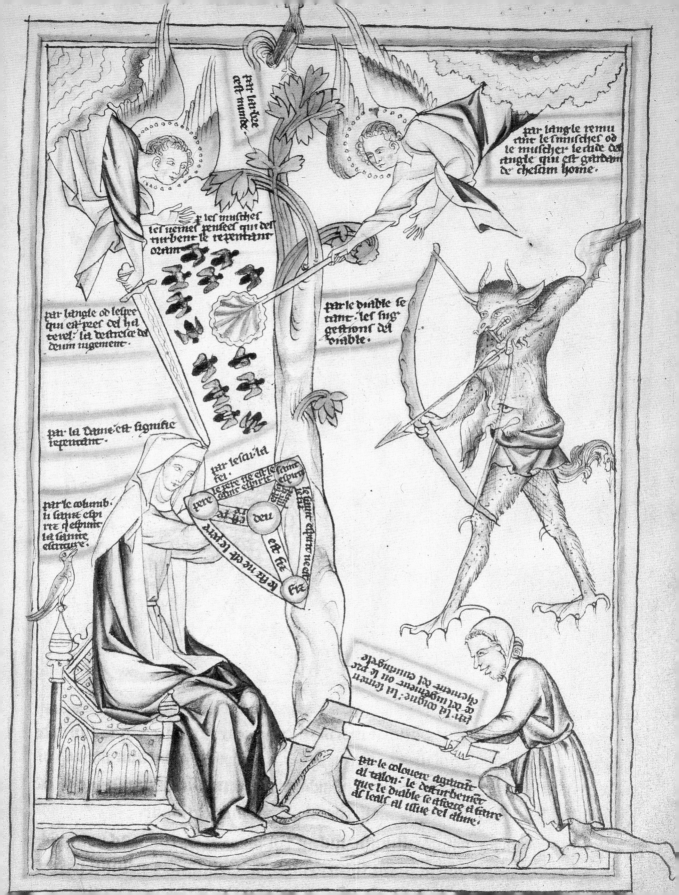

par le mûde cest mûde.

par langle remû...
rint le s mûnches od
le mûscher· le tide des
angle qui est gardain
de chest[m] home.

...r les mûschet
les uernes penses qui dest
urbent le repentant
...rum·

par langle od lespre
qui est pres del hil
terel· les destresse del
deum tugement·

par le diable se
tant· les sug
gestions des
diable·

par la Dame est signifie
repentant·

par le columb
li saint espir
rre q eschint
les saintes
escruture·

par lesai· la
fei· le pere ne est le saint
pere ne est le saint esprit·
al tir deu
le saint esprit ne est
est le fiz
le fiz ne est le pere·

par la colume· la lumer
de l'ugement· on il pur
chemine des cunduuit·

par le colouere agruut...
al talon· le desturbemer
que le diable se attace el sune
al lealt· il issue del ame·

– III –
🌸 MARGERY KEMPE 🌸
born c. 1373

> '... *O*UR MERCIFUL LORD visited this
> creature with abundant tears of contrition
> day by day ... those who before had
> respected her, afterwards most sharply
> rebuked her ... She was so used to being
> slandered and reproved, to being chided and
> rebuked by the world for grace and virtue
> with which she was endued through the
> strength of the Holy Spirit, that it was to her
> a kind of solace and comfort when she
> suffered any distress for the love of God.'
>
> 🌸 THE BOOK OF MARGERY KEMPE

Opposite: An allegorical depiction of the struggle between virtue and vice for control of the individual soul.

MARGERY KEMPE WAS BORN IN ABOUT 1373, into very comfortable circumstances. Her father, John Burnham, was a wealthy and successful businessman and a prominent member of the civic community of King's Lynn, or Bishop's Lynn as it was in those days. In the fourteenth century Lynn was a busy, thriving port situated on the east coast. Margery's father represented the town in parliament between 1364 and 1384 and he was also an alderman of the Guild of the Holy Trinity, a wealthy, prestigious and exclusive trade organization in Lynn.

She tells us nothing at all about her childhood, but begins her narrative very abruptly with her marriage and the birth of her first child. Her husband was John Kempe, also a merchant of Lynn (possibly a brewer), but rather less prominent and successful than her father. In any case he was a good, kind husband to Margery. Childbirth was notoriously dangerous for women in those primitive and unsanitary days, and the birth of Margery's first child was a difficult one. She had been sick all through the pregnancy and her labour was agonizing. It caused in

A prosperous merchant rides out, proudly displaying his sword. Margery's father was someone like this, a successful business man, and she did not let her husband forget it!

her a physical and emotional crisis. Fearing that she was dying, she sent for a priest to confess her sins:

Then she sent for her confessor, for she had something on her conscience that she had never before disclosed to anyone in all her life ... But when she came to the point of telling the thing that she had concealed for so long, her confessor was a little too hasty, and began sharply to reprove her before she had fully said what she wanted to, and then she would say nothing more in spite of anything he could do. And soon after, because of the dread she had of damnation on the one hand, and his sharp reproving of her on the other, this creature went out of her mind and was amazingly disturbed and tormented by spirits for half a year, eight weeks and odd days. And in this time she saw, it seemed to her, devils opening their mouths all ablaze with burning flames of fire, as if they would have swallowed her up; sometimes they pawed at her, or threatened her, or pulled her about by night and by day... She would have killed herself many times, as they stirred her to, and would have been damned with them in hell. To witness this, she bit her own hands so violently that the scars could be seen for the rest of her life; and also she pitilessly tore the skin of her body near her heart with her nails, for she had no other weapon, and she would have done something even worse, if she had not been tied up and forcibly restrained both night and day... (Chapter 1)

What this unmentionable secret sin was, she doesn't tell us, but we can guess from the evidence of other parts of her story that it was sexual in nature. The illness brought on by Margery's guilt and terror continued for eight months. The Middle Ages were not noted for the humane treatment of the mentally ill, and it says much for her husband's humanity and fondness for her that he kept his young wife at home and constantly watched over. Then, one day when her guardians were out of the room for a while, she had a vision:

... our merciful Lord Jesus Christ, who is always to be trusted, his name always to be worshipped, who never forsakes his servants in time of need, appeared to this creature in the form of a man. He was the most beautiful, most seemly, and most amiable man...He was clad in a mantle of purple silk, and sat at her bedside, looking at her with so blessed a face that she at once felt strengthened in her spirits. Then he said to her these words: 'Daughter, why have you forsaken me, for I have never forsaken you?' As soon as he had spoken these words, she saw how the air opened up and grew as bright as lightning, and he ascended into the air, not suddenly or

hastily, but gently and gradually, so that she could clearly see him in the air until it closed upon him again. Afterwards this creature performed all her responsibilities wisely and soberly enough, except that she did not truly acknowledge our Lord's power to draw us to him. (Chapter 1)

Margery was grateful to God for bringing her back to herself, but was not yet able to give up her worldly life. She took great pleasure in showy dressing, and liked to make people stare at her with her fashionably 'slashed' hoods and cloaks where, as she tells us, the slashed top layer of material revealed a contrasting colour beneath. Her husband tried to remonstrate with her to be more moderate in her dress and leave her proud ways; she merely retorted sharply that 'she came from a worthy family; he should never have married her, ...and therefore she would keep up the honour of her family, whatever anyone said.' With ruthless honesty, Margery confesses that she was immediately jealous if any of her neighbours were as well-dressed as she was, and that her whole desire was to be respected by people. She had not learned her lesson; but God was not finished with her yet. She decided to go into business for herself 'out of sheer greed, and in order to keep up her pride' – in other words, to provide her with her own money to spend on her extravagant clothes – and set up as a brewer. It was not all that unusual for middle-class medieval women to run a local business in this way.

She was one of the greatest brewers in the town of [Lynn] for three or four years, until she lost a great deal of money, for she had never had any experience in that business. For however skilled her men were, and

A wedding scene. Note the father of the bride handing over the dowry. Margery's father was a successful man and she would have had a generous dowry.

however knowledgeable in brewing, suddenly nothing would go right for them. For when the ale had as fine a head of froth on it as anyone could wish to see, the froth would unexpectedly go flat, and all the ale was lost, in one brewing after another, so that her men were ashamed of their failure and would not stay and work for her any more. (Chapter 2)

Margery with innocent egotism attributed the failure of her brewing business to God's intention of humbling her pride. She decided to give up brewing. She also asked her husband's pardon because she had not taken his advice before, and explained to him that she was being punished for her pride, and wanted to put everything right. This did not prevent her, however, from setting up another ill-fated new business: 'She had a horse-mill. She got herself two good horses and a man to grind people's corn, and in this way she was confident of making a living.' However, the horses refused to work and this was interpreted as a miracle designed to humble her. So, at any rate, thought her contemporaries, for a rumour started that neither man nor beast would work for her, and that she was accursed.

The Long Road to Conversion

Margery realized that she must take drastic steps to amend her life:

Then this creature, seeing all these adversities coming upon her from every side, thought they were the scourges of our Lord, punishing her for her sin. Then she asked God for mercy, and forsook her pride and her covetousness, and her desire for worldly reputation, and did great bodily penance, and began to enter the way of everlasting life. (Chapter 2)

The reasoning Margery shows here set the pattern for her future life as a lay person dedicated to religion. She became convinced that everything that happened to her

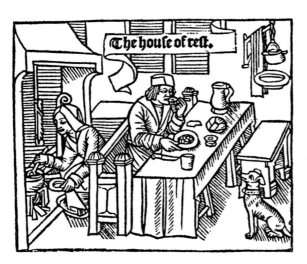

A woman serves a man at table. Medieval wives had a subservient role, but Margery's husband was kind and indulgent towards her.

was personally arranged by God to contribute to her salvation, 'for she knew very well that she had sinned greatly against God, and that she deserved far more shame and sorrow than any man could cause her, and contempt in this world was the right way towards heaven, for Christ himself chose that way.' Therefore she welcomed every experience of suffering or fear, because it would bring her nearer to heaven. Margery felt she had been granted a personal vision of paradise:

One night, as this creature lay in bed with her husband, she heard a sound of music so sweet and so pleasurable that she thought she had been in paradise. At once she jumped out of bed and said,

'Alas, that ever I sinned! It is full merry in heaven.' The melody was so sweet that it surpassed all the melody that could be heard in this world, beyond comparison, and it caused this creature when she afterwards heard any mirth or melody to shed very plentiful and abundant tears of high devotion, with great sobs and sighs for the bliss of heaven, and fearless of the shames and contempt of this wretched world. (Chapter 3)

A housewife using a butter churn. Margery probably supervised, rather than participated in, this sort of activity.

After being granted this glimpse of heavenly joy, the nature of Margery's religious experience was characterized permanently by these noisy and uncontrollable fits of crying. She describes how, in addition to this sense of loss after glimpsing a vision of wonderful happiness, she felt the same overwhelming grief at how her sinfulness had personally wounded our Lord, after all his kindness to her: 'And this creature had contrition and great compunction, with plentiful tears and much loud and violent sobbing, for her sins and for her unkindness towards her maker.' Her plentiful and continual weeping and crying was, of course, very annoying to other people, and continued to be a source of gratifying martyrdom to Margery for the rest of her life. As a hysterical person she almost certainly could not control these emotional outbursts, although this does not mean they were unwelcome to her. The public grieving generated even more attention than all her fine and fashionable clothes. Margery also practised more conventional forms of self-imposed penance:

She gave herself up to much fasting and keeping of vigil...And then she was slandered and reproved by many people because she led so strict a life. She got herself a hair-cloth from a kiln – the sort that malt is dried on – and put it inside her gown as discreetly and secretly as she could, so that her husband should not notice it. And nor did he, although she lay beside him every night in bed and wore the hair shirt every day, and bore him children during that time. (Chapter 3)

And there was one more thing that Margery wanted to complete her conversion to a religious life and dedicate herself to God – celibacy. Given that she was still married to, and living with, her husband, this was a tall order. During the first twenty years of marriage, she says later, she bore him fourteen children, whom she does not mention again – probably few of them survived to adulthood. She had now lost all her desire for her husband – and she admits that they had previously had a terrific sex life – and began to badger him to give up his conjugal rights:

And so...this creature advised her husband to live chaste and said that they had often, she well knew, displeased God by their inordinate love, and the great delight that each of them had in using the other's body, and now it would be a good thing if by mutual consent they punished and chastised themselves by abstaining from the lust of their bodies.Her husband agreed that it would be a good thing to do, but he couldn't manage it yet – he would do so when God willed. And so he used her as he had done before, he would not desist. (Chapter 3)

The Final Temptation

Margery was about thirty-six, still attractive, still bearing children, having previously enjoyed an active sexual life, when she decided to give it up to turn to God. Unfortunately she then fell into the dangerous trap of over-confidence:

> *She could well endure fasting – it did not trouble her. She hated the joys of the world. She felt no rebellion in her flesh. She was so strong – as she thought – that she feared no devil in hell, for she performed such great bodily penance. She thought that she loved God more than he loved her. She was smitten with the deadly wound of vainglory and felt it not ...* (Chapter 4)

Margery then confesses with astonishing frankness the story of the final obstacle to be overcome on her road to salvation. It was not so easy for her to shrug off the seductive call of the body. Here is her account of the humiliating experience of rejection that contributed towards her final crisis of self-doubt:

> *...it so happened that a man whom she liked said to her ... that, for anything, he would sleep with her and enjoy the lust of his body, and that she should not withstand him, for if he could not have his desire then, he said, he would have it another time instead – she would have no choice. He really did this to test what she would do, but she thought he meant it in earnest, and said very little in reply. So they parted then and both went to hear evensong ... This woman was so troubled by the man's words that she could not ... think any other good thought, but was more disturbed than she ever was before ... This creature was so troubled and vexed all night that she did not know what she could do. She lay beside her husband, and to have intercourse with him was so disgusting to her that she could not bear it, ... But all the time she was tortured [by the desire] to sin with the other man, because he had spoken to her. At last – through the importunings of temptation and a lack of discretion – she was overcome, and consented in her mind, and went to the man to know if he would then consent to have her. And he said he would not for all the wealth in this world; he would rather be chopped up as small as meat for the pot. She went away all ashamed and confused in herself, seeing his steadfastness, and her own instability ... then she half fell into despair. (Chapter 4)*

A medieval interpretation of Christ's death. Margery had a passionate desire to travel to Jerusalem to see the Holy Lands for herself.

After this particularly cruel and stupid man had led her on and then so brutally repulsed her, Margery was plunged into a long spiritual crisis, in which she loathed and despised herself so much that she could not really believe in God's love for her. She confessed this sin and did penance for it, but still had such a low opinion of herself that she could see no way forward, and became locked in a cycle of lustful feelings, followed by self-disgust and despair. She could not forgive herself, and could not feel herself worthy of God's forgiveness. This continued for about a year; then, suddenly, God's love took her by surprise. She was kneeling in St

John's Chapel within the church of St Margaret in Lynn as usual, weeping hard and praying for forgiveness, when suddenly Christ 'ravished her spirit' and spoke directly to her. This speech marks the beginning of a new relationship with God for Margery, in which she can confide in him, explain her problems, ask questions, and receive absolutely explicit answers and advice about what to do next:

> *Therefore, I command you, boldly call me Jesus, your love, for I am your love and shall be your love without end. And, daughter, you have a hair-shirt on your back. I want you to leave off wearing it, and I shall give you a hair-shirt in your heart which shall please me much more than all the hair-shirts in the world. But also, my beloved daughter, you must give up that which you love best in this world, and that is the eating of meat. And instead of meat you shall eat my flesh and my blood, that is the true body of Christ in the sacrament of the altar. This is my will, daughter, that you receive my body every Sunday, and I shall cause so much grace to flow into you that everyone shall marvel at it. (Chapter 5)*

It was then very unusual for people to communicate every Sunday – four times a year was the norm. She must also go and report herself to 'the anchorite at the Preaching Friars' and tell him what Christ has said to her. This she does, and the anchorite, deeply moved, tells her, 'Daughter, you are sucking even at Christ's breast.' This man, Master Robert, became Margery's confessor. After three years of isolation, doubt, guilt, and loneliness, the joy and relief with which Margery greets this new revelation of Christ's love for her are palpable. She finds from then on that her trust in God does not fail, and this is intensely consoling for her, especially when she meets, as she often does, with distrust and hostility from other people. Whenever she opens her mind to God she is rewarded with vivid dramatic visions in which she seems to participate in scenes from the Gospels and can communicate directly with God, Christ, the Virgin Mary and various saints.

God's Messenger

At this point in her career, Margery began to travel about England visiting churchmen in different cities and communities. Her husband accompanied her on these journeys. Margery tells us that her husband was generally very good to her and supported her whenever she provoked hostility by her constant noisy crying, but there were times when even he couldn't stand it, and abandoned her. She tells of one occasion when she was visiting Canterbury, when 'she was greatly reproved and despised because she wept so much – both by monks and priests, and by secular men, nearly all day, both morning and afternoon – and so much so that her husband went away from her as if he had not known her, and left her alone among them.' On this occasion she excited such anger that some people began calling out for her to be burnt as a heretic and a Lollard. Margery was very frightened as the mob grew and their taunts became uglier; she prayed to God and was shortly rescued by two young men who conducted her back to her lodging house.

On these trips around England, Margery also met with very sympathetic treatment; many people considered her weeping a sign of grace, and were very moved to hear her speak publicly about God's love; for example, she tells how in London, 'many worthy men wanted to hear her converse, for her conversation was so much to do with the love of God that those who heard it were often moved to weep'. She was often received graciously by eminent churchmen – including the Archbishop of Canterbury, who was very kind to her even after she complained to

A couple enjoying the delights of the bedchamber. Margery admitted that she and her husband had a terrific sex life before she decided that celibacy was essential to her salvaltion!

MARGERY ❧ KEMPE ❧

A wonderfully striking image of Christ in Majesty. Such powerful images must have inspired Margery when the world seemed to disapprove of her more expressive forms of worship.

him that he was allowing his servants to use bad language and oaths. She visited bishops, abbots, priests, monks, and other notable religious figures. She visited the famous anchoress Dame Julian of Norwich, and reported their conversation. She seems almost to have been testing herself all the time to make sure that her revelations were from God and not the devil. She described her conversations with God in which, as she says, 'the Father of Heaven conversed with her soul as plainly and certainly as one friend speaks to another through bodily speech' to Julian, 'to find out if there were any deception in them, for the anchoress was expert in such things and could give good advice'. Julian reassured Margery at some length that her tears were genuinely prompted by grace and were the gift of the Holy Spirit. They spent several days together 'talking of the love of our Lord Jesus Christ'. The voice of Julian, so familiar to us from her writings in *Revelations of Divine Love*, is uncannily accurately expressed in the account that Margery gives.

Much of what God says to Margery regarding herself is of a very loving and reassuring nature; he constantly tells her that he loves her, that he will never forsake her, that he forgives all her sins, that her place in heaven is assured, and so on. After her long years of agonizing self-doubt and self-hatred, it is entirely understandable that Margery should find this spontaneous kindness and love almost unbearably moving: 'Then this creature lay still, weeping and sobbing as if her heart would burst for the sweetness of speech that our Lord spoke to her soul'.

Often, however, God's communications to Margery took the form of practical revelations more in the nature of prophecies – whether a particular person was going to live or die, whether they would be saved or damned. Margery found these visions much more difficult to deal with, and also harder to trust. She seems to have had a very good nose for sniffing out frauds and charlatans even without God's help. The priest who wrote her book down, for example, recorded voluntarily how she had been accurate in her judgment of a very handsome and plausible young man who had borrowed some money from him. The young man went away, promising to return and pay the money back in a few days. Margery 'said she supposed that he would not see him any more, and nor did he ever again. And then he regretted that he had not done as she advised'.

The Vow of Chastity

After three years of her dedication to the religious life and her closer relationship with God, Margery's husband had still not agreed to her request for chastity, although she managed at one point to frighten him into leaving her alone. She finally succeeded in persuading her husband to take a vow of chastity in 1413, when she was about forty years old. Margery describes in detail the crucial scene in which she finally got her wish, in which Christ helps her out with the finer points of the negotiation. Margery is remembering this a good twenty years after it took place, but it remains fresh and vivid, conveying very powerfully both her husband's irritation with her and his great fondness for her:

A woodcut showing a medieval friar on horseback. Friars were qualified to hear confessions. Margery was instructed by God to choose a friar who had enclosed himself in a cell as her confessor.

It happened one Friday, Midsummer Eve, in very hot weather – as this creature was coming from York carrying a bottle of beer in her hand, and her husband a cake tucked inside his clothes against his chest – that her husband asked his wife this question: 'Margery, if there came a man with a sword who would strike off my head unless I made love to you as I used to do before, tell me on your conscience – for you say you will not lie – whether you would allow my head to be cut off, or else allow me to make love with you again, as I did at one time?'

MARGERY KEMPE

'Alas, sir,' said she, 'why are you raising this matter, when we have been chaste for these past eight weeks?'

'Because I want to know the truth of your heart.'

And then she said with great sorrow, 'Truly, I would rather see you being killed, than that we should turn back to our uncleanness.'

And he replied, 'You are no good wife.'

Then they went on towards Bridlington… And as they came by a cross her husband sat down under the cross, calling his wife to him and saying these words to her:

'Margery, grant me my desire, and I shall grant you your desire. My first desire is that we shall still lie together in one bed as we have done before; the second, that you shall pay my debts before you go to Jerusalem; and the third, that you shall eat and drink with me on Fridays as you used to do.'

'No sir,' she said, 'I will never agree to break my Friday fast as long as I live.'

'Well,' he said, 'in that case I'm going to have sex with you again.'

(Chapter 11)

An illustration of a monk and nun travelling, from the Romance of the Rose. Margery, like many medieval pilgrims, travelled extensively.

She begged him to allow her to say her prayers, and he kindly allowed it. Margery then consulted Christ, pointing out to him that if it were not for her need to obey his direct command about not eating meat on Fridays, she could now easily make an agreement not to have sex with her husband any more. However, she will never disobey Christ's will. Margery tells us that Christ then informed her that his command to her to fast was in fact just a negotiating ploy; she can now agree to her husband's terms, as he no longer wishes her to fast, 'and therefore I command you in the name of Jesus to eat and drink as your husband does.'

An illustration from the famous penitential manual La Somme le Roi *by Friar Laurent, showing devotional acts.*

> Then this creature thanked our Lord Jesus Christ for his grace and his goodness, and afterwards got up and went to her husband, saying to him, 'Sir, if you please, you shall grant me my desire, and you shall have your desire. Grant me that you will not come into my bed, and I grant you that I will pay your debts before I go to Jerusalem. And make my body free to God, so that you never make any claim on me requesting any conjugal debt after this day as long as you live – and I shall eat and drink on Fridays at your bidding.' Then her husband replied to her, 'May your body be as freely available to God as it has been to me.'
>
> This creature thanked God greatly, rejoicing that she had her desire, praying her husband that they should say three paternosters in worship of the Trinity for the great grace that had been granted them. And so they did, kneeling under the cross, and afterwards they ate and drank together in great gladness of spirit. This was on a Friday, on Midsummer's Eve.

(Chapter 11)

Margery the Pilgrim

This mention of Jerusalem is the first indication we have that Margery intends to go on pilgrimage to that city. It was the longest, most arduous, and most dangerous pilgrimage that could be undertaken from England. Later she mentions that she had wanted to see all the places where Christ suffered his passion and death for some considerable time, and that two years before she actually went, Christ commanded her to go to Rome, Jerusalem, and Santiago de Compostela, 'and she would gladly have gone, but she had no money to go with'. When she asked our Lord how she was going to obtain the necessary money to travel to these

MARGERY ❧ KEMPE ❧

distant places, he simply replied that he would send her friends to protect and guide her, and would provide for her in every country.

Margery does not mention it, but what may have made the pilgrimage to Jerusalem a possibility was the death of her father in 1413, as he probably left her some money. True to her word, she paid her husband's debts, and made arrangements to travel with her maidservant and a confessor, a supposedly holy man who was a friend of her confessor in Lynn (he, being an anchorite, could never leave his cell). She joined a company of other pilgrims. But this is where Margery's problems began. Her fellow-pilgrims were annoyed because she wept so much and spoke about God all the time. They looked on their pilgrimage as package tour to foreign climes; real religious feelings embarrassed them. They seem to have been fairly typical of fifteenth-century people in the nature of their religious beliefs. 'And so they rebuked her shamefully and chided her harshly, and said they would not put up with her as her husband did when she was at home in England.' Worse, they turned her confessor and her maidservant against her. Her confessor, displeased because she ate no meat, no longer defended her peculiarities against the others, but joined in their rude treatment of her. She became the butt of everyone's cruel jokes, and no one would stand up for her. It was essential for Margery to travel with them for safety, but her group continued to ostracize and mock her:

Medieval travel writing – an illustration to one of Robert Langton's accounts of his pilgrimage to Santiago de Compostela and the places of interest along the way.

> *They cut her gown so short that it only came a little below her knee, and made her put on some white canvas in a kind of sacking apron, so that she would be taken for a fool, and people would not make much of her or hold her in any repute. They made her sit at the end of the table below all the others, so that she scarcely dared speak a word. But in spite of all their malice, she was held in more esteem than they were, wherever they went. And the good man of the house where they were staying, even though she sat at the end of the table, would always do whatever he could to cheer her up before them all and sent her bits and pieces from his own plate, and that really annoyed her companions.*

In Constance, Margery discovered a papal legate, an English friar and, as she used to do on her travels round

England, she sought him out and told him the story of her life. This man was impressed by Margery and very kindly supported her against the cruelty and pettiness of her group, who invited him to dinner so that they could complain about her. They wanted him 'to order her to eat meat as they did, and leave off her weeping, and that she should not talk so much of holiness.' Then the worthy doctor said:

> No sirs, I will not make her eat meat while she can abstain and be the better disposed to love our Lord … As for her weeping, it is not in my power to restrain it, for it is the gift of the Holy Ghost. As for her talking, I will ask her to stop until she comes somewhere that people will hear her more gladly than you do.' The company was extremely angry. They gave her over to the legate and said absolutely that they would have nothing more to do with her. He very kindly and benevolently received her as though she had been his mother… And the legate made all arrangements for this creature, and organized for her the exchange of her English money into foreign money. (Chapter 27)

A man bargains with a ship's master for a place on the ship. Note the chest beside the woman – each pilgrim had to make his or her own travel arrangements.

Then Margery fell in with an elderly man from Devonshire called William Weaver, who undertook to escort her. She travelled with William as far as Bologna, without the slightest trouble, meeting nothing but kindness on the way. At Bologna she met up with her group again, and they offered to have her back in their party, provided that she would promise not to talk about the Gospels all the time but to 'sit and make merry, like us, at all meals'. Margery accepted, until they got to Venice, but then she recited a Gospel text at dinner and broke her promise.

A thriving travel business in ferrying pilgrims to and from the port of Jaffa had grown up in Venice. Pilgrim ships usually sailed from there in the late spring or early summer; this group of pilgrims had arrived in January and had to wait thirteen weeks before they could book their passage. It was usual for a group to negotiate directly with individual captains to get the best price for their journey. We know from the accounts left by other pilgrims, though Margery doesn't mention it, what conditions on board a pilgrim galley were like. The following is taken from an account left by Friar Felix Fabri, of a journey made in 1484. The pilgrims had a 'cabin' below deck, which was a large open chamber stretching the whole length of the ship. Every bit of it was filled with berths, so that when filled the pilgrims lay like sardines in a can, their heads towards the side of the ship and their feet towards the centre. Along the central aisle were placed the pilgrims'

MARGERY
❦ KEMPE ❦

trunks and chests, where they kept their clothes and belongings. The wise and experienced pilgrim would take care to provide herself with her own pots and pans, dishes, plates, cups and other utensils in addition to a chest for clothes, barrels for water and wine, and bedding. Conditions on board were very cramped and totally insanitary; all ships were infested with rats and mice and, living in such crowded quarters, it was also impossible to escape fleas. Friar Felix commented that 'there is among all the occupations of the seafarers one which, albeit loathesome, is yet very common, daily and necessary – I mean the hunting and catching of lice and vermin. Unless a man spends several hours in this work when he is on a pilgrimage, he will have but unquiet slumbers.' Other ways of occupying the long hours on the month-long sea voyage included gambling and drinking for the less godly and more pleasure-seeking element; some took violent exercise, lifting weights or climbing the rigging, while others spent a vast amount of their time praying or meditating and preparing for the pilgrimage ahead.

Since we can guess how Margery would be spending a large part of each day, we can sympathize a little with her group when they decided that on no account could they bear to be in the same small, crowded ship with her, and went to arrange their passage without her. Poor Margery tagged along behind, bought herself some bedding from the same supplier, and came to see them, 'intending to sail with them in that ship which they had engaged'. However, afterwards while she was meditating, she received some crucial information:

... our Lord warned her in her mind that she should not sail in that ship, and he assigned her another ship, a galley, that she should sail in. Then she told this to some of her company, and they told it to others of their party, and then they dared not sail in the ship which they had arranged.
(Chapter 28)

It so happened that God had previously promised Margery that she should go and return in safety, and in particular that 'no Englishman shall die in the ship that you are in'. Margery must have shared this information with her group who, like most fifteenth-century people, were extremely superstitious. Even though they found Margery a dreadful nuisance, they didn't dare not believe in her. Even so, her

Pilgrims approaching the city gates, where they will bargain for admittance and accommodation. Illustration from Sir John Mandeville's Travels, *another fifteenth-century travelogue.*

persecutions did not stop; on board ship they locked up her bedclothes, and one of them stole a sheet from her and said it was his (and he was a priest!)

At last, they reached Jerusalem. This was an overwhelming experience for Margery. She was granted powerful visions, first seeing the heavenly Jerusalem suspended in the air above the earthly city, and afterwards when they were touring the sites of the Passion, seeing the events of it unfold before her eyes:

> *... this creature wept and sobbed as plenteously as though she had seen our Lord with her bodily eyes suffering his Passion at that time ... And when they came up on to the Mount of Calvary, she fell down because she could not stand or kneel, but writhed and wrestled with her body, spreading her arms out wide, and cried with a loud voice as though her heart would have burst apart... And this kind of crying lasted for many years after this time... (Chapter 28)*

Margery and her companions spent three weeks in Jerusalem visiting the Holy Places. Her travelling companions continued to be beastly to her and they even tried to leave her behind whenever they went on an excursion, but the friars of the Church of the Holy Sepulchre were kind to her and took her in. Even the Saracens could see that she was holy and were good to her. After this they set off back home. On the return voyage some of her group became ill; she was able to reassure them of the promise she had received from Christ that no English person would die in the ship she was in, and so it proved. Still, when they got safely to Venice, 'her fellow countrymen abandoned her and went off, leaving her alone. And some of them said that they would not go with her for a hundred pounds.' Margery had intended to go to Rome on her way back to England, but now she had no companions with whom to travel. She found a very poor Irishman with a humpback, whose name was Richard, and she persuaded him to accompany her, which he did very faithfully, finding companions for her when he was obliged to follow his calling and beg during the day. They arrived in about September 1414, and soon met up with her original companions. She stayed in Rome for about six months, and then returned home to England. Her husband came and met her in Norwich and escorted her back to Lynn, where she fell seriously ill for a while. As she was recovering she decided that she must go on pilgrimage again, this time to Santiago de Compostela in northern Spain, before she died. Once more she was destitute and in debt; but once more the Lord told her not to worry, for he would provide for her, and Margery accomplished her wish in the summer of 1417.

Margery in Danger

The early fifteenth century was the period when the Lollard heresy was very much on people's minds in England; the famous Lollard, Sir John Oldcastle, was captured, tried, condemned and burnt to death in December 1417. Margery was so conspicuous and so outspoken that her friends feared she would be seized and burnt. She found herself under suspicion of heresy. She was arrested and thrown into gaol at Leicester on her way home from Bristol after her trip to Santiago. By this time, however, Margery had become so accustomed to dealing with violent hostility from other people and answering their accusations that she was able to answer patiently and reasonably all the questions she was asked by highly educated clerics who were trying to catch her out in some unorthodoxy in her religious views or practices. She was so calm, so strong in her conviction, and so clearly not heretical that the Mayor of Leicester was obliged to release her, though he insisted that she get a letter from the Bishop of Lincoln absolving him of the responsibility for any harm she might do after he had let her go.

Margery next went to York, where she had to face an even more fearful ordeal. She was publicly examined in the chapterhouse at York Minster on the articles of faith. Despite returning nothing but satisfactory answers, she was summoned to appear before the Archbishop himself on a subsequent day, and only the support of the townspeople (for once) prevented her from being thrown into prison. Her courage in what must have been a very frightening situation was remarkable; but Margery's faith in God gave her a huge reserve of strength:

> *On the next day she was brought into the Archbishop's chapel, and many of the Archbishop's household came there scorning her, calling her*

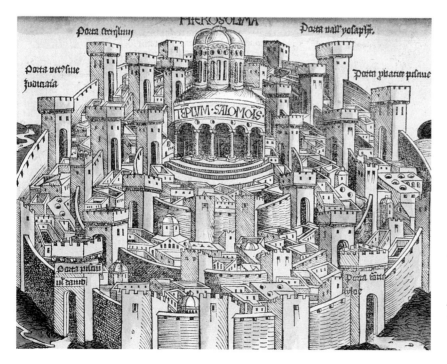

A fifteenth-century engraving of the city of Jerusalem, where Margery went on her first and longest pilgrimage, showing the Temple of Soloman and the city wall and gates.

MARGERY ❧ KEMPE ❧

'Lollard' and 'heretic', and swore many a horrible oath that she should be burned. And she ... replied to them, 'Sirs, I fear you will be burned in hell without end, unless you correct yourselves of your swearing of oaths, for you do not keep the commandments of God...' Then they went away, as if they were ashamed...At last the Archbishop came into the chapel with his clerics and said she should be fettered, for she was a false heretic, and then she said, 'I am no heretic, nor shall you prove me one.' The Archbishop went away and left her standing alone.

The Archbishop returned with his clerics and while the court was settling Margery had one of her really major crying fits.

When her crying was passed, she came before the Archbishop and felldown on her knees, the Archbishop saying very roughly to her, 'Why do you weep so, woman?' She answering said, 'Sir, you shall wish some day that you had wept as sorely as I.' Then the Archbishop said to her: 'I am told very bad things about you. I hear it said that you are a very wicked woman.' And she replied, 'Sir, I also hear it said that you are a wicked man. And if you are as wicked as people say, you will never get to heaven, unless you amend while you are here.' Then he said very roughly, 'Why you! ... What do people say of me?' She answered, 'Other people, sir, can tell you well enough.'

St James the Greater, the patron saint of Santiago de Compostela, where God commanded Margey to go on pilgrimage. In this image he carries the pilgrim's gourd and wears the pilgrim's hat.

The Archbishop offered to let her go if she would swear to leave his diocese immediately. Margery refused, having not completed her visits yet. Then he said she could have permission to visit Bridlington if she would swear 'not to teach people or call them to account in my diocese.' Margery refused again, saying that she certainly would 'rebuke those who swear great oaths wherever I go'. A cleric then quoted St Paul against her, who said that no woman should preach (I Corinthians xiv, 34-5). Margery replied with spirit : 'I do not preach, sir; I do not go into any pulpit. I use only conversation and good words, and that I will do while I live.' Then another learned doctor told the Archbishop that Margery had told him 'the worst tale about priests that I ever heard.' The Archbishop asked to hear the tale, and Margery duly repeated it. It concerns a priest who, when lost in a wood, found a garden to shelter in where there was a pear-tree covered in beautiful blossoms. Along came a bear, shook all the blossoms off the tree and ate them, and then 'when he had eaten them, turned his tail towards the priest and discharged them out again at his rear end.' The priest subsequently meets a pilgrim who explains to him that the meaning of the vision is that he the priest wastes and squanders the flowers of grace in the sacraments, and mass, because he is careless and worldly and more interested in beer, money, food and women than in doing his job properly, 'thus, through your own misconduct, just like the loathesome bear, you devour and destroy the flowers and blossoms of virtuous living, to your

*St Peter shown as an
evangelist carrying the key
to heaven. In the Middle
Ages going on pilgrimage,
as Margery did, was
commonly thought to be a
way of achieving salvation.*

endless damnation.' Luckily for Margery, the crusty old Archbishop rather liked
this story, and giving one of his men five shillings to escort her, blessed her and let
her go. Unfortunately, she had only got as far as the Humber when she was
arrested again, this time by the Duke of Bedford's men, and found herself hauled
back before the Archbishop. 'Then the Archbishop said to this creature 'What,
woman, have you come back again? I would gladly be rid of you!' This time she
was even accused of being a Lollard spy, the daughter of Sir John Oldcastle,
travelling about the country delivering letters. But the Archbishop declared that all
the charges were nonsense, and Margery was sent home to Lynn.

Margery's Final Journey

She stayed at home for about fifteen years. During this period Margery saw the
great fire of Lynn in 1421, helped a poor woman who had gone out of her mind
after childbirth as she had once done, and nursed her husband. Now over sixty , he
had a bad fall downstairs, and suffered serious head injuries. They were living
apart at the time, and Margery was blamed for neglecting him. She prayed to God
that he should live, and God, who never seems to have given Margery anything but
sound good sense, said that he would, but that she must look after him:

*Then she took her husband home with her and looked after him for years
afterwards, as long as he lived. She had very much trouble with him, for*

in his last days he turned childish and lacked reason, so that he could not go to a stool to relieve himself, or else he would not, but like a child discharged his excrement into his linen clothes as he sat there by the fire or at the table – wherever it was, he would spare no place. And so her labour was all the greater, in washing and wringing, and so were her expenses for keeping a fire going. All this hindered her a very great deal from her contemplation, so that many times she would have disliked her work, except that she thought to herself how she in her young days had had very many delectable thoughts, physical lust, and inordinate love for his body. And therefore she was glad to be punished by means of the same body, and took it much the more easily, and served him and helped him, she thought, as she would have done Christ himself.

John died in 1431. All this time Margery had also been getting her book written down for her, probably by her son, who had married a German woman but had come back to live in Lynn. Shortly before the death of her husband, this son had also tragically been taken ill and died. His German wife stayed with Margery for eighteen months, but at last wanted to return to her home in Prussia, not least to see her little girl, whom she had left behind with her family. Margery decided to go with her, and so in 1433, at the age of sixty, she set off once more on her travels. Originally she had intended only to see her daughter-in-law onto a ship, but the Lord instructed her to go with her, so she did (despite her daughter-in-law begging her not to!) This was very brave, given her advanced age and the certainty that she would encounter abuse from people in addition to all the usual hardships of foreign travel. She visited Danzig, from where she went to see the Holy Blood at Wilsnak, and our Lady's smock and other relics at Aachen, before returning to England. As before, she endured many hardships, but also a great deal of kindness. She made it home unscathed, although, she tells us, she went in constant fear of being raped.

Once she got home, her main concern was to get her book written down. She persuaded a priest to read over the portion that had been written by her son before his death. However, the priest complained that the language was neither English nor 'Dutch' but a mixture of the two, and that the handwriting was very difficult to decipher. He was most reluctant to involve himself in what looked like a very long and difficult project; but Margery persuaded him, and he began in July 1435:

When the priest first began to write this book his eyes failed, so that he could not see to form his letters and could not see to mend his pen ... He complained to the creature about his troubles. She said his enemy was envious of his good deed and would hinder him if he might (i.e. the devil), and she bade him do as well as God would give him grace and not give up. When he came back to his book again, he could see as well, he thought, as he ever did before both by daylight and by candlelight.

*After her travels Margery
devotedly nursed her husband
in his declining years. She
viewed his incontinence and
dementia as a penance for
their earlier sexual pleasures.*

Gradually he re-wrote and finished the first book, and on 28 April 1438 he began
to add the second book, which deals with Margery's final pilgrimage. The book
ends with a long prayer in which Margery summarizes her beliefs and way of life.

In 1438, too, Margery was admitted as a member of the Guild of the Holy
Trinity in Lynn, a great honour, which shows that at last the people of Lynn had
come to feel proud of their strange mystic. There are no further records of her life,
and we do not know when she died; in 1521 however when the printer Henry
Pepwell re-issued Wynkyn de Worde's seven-page leaflet about Margery, *A Shorte
Treatyse of Contemplatyon Taught by our Lorde Ihesu Cryste, Taken out of the Boke of
Margerie Kempe of Lynne*, he states that Margery was 'a devout anchoress'. Was he
making this up, or had Margery in the final years of her life given up the prospect
of ever travelling again, and dedicated herself exclusively to God in a cell attached
to her beloved St Margaret's Church? We will never know.

– IV –
❦ HILDEGARD of BINGEN ❦
1098–1179

> '*A*T LAST, in the time that followed, I saw a mystic and wondrous vision, such that all my womb was convulsed and my body's sensory powers extinguished, because my knowledge was transmuted into another mode, as if I no longer knew myself. And from God's inspiration as it were, drops of gentle rain splashed into the knowledge of my soul.'
>
> ❦ HILDEGARD DESCRIBES A CRUCIAL VISION, THEODORIC OF ECHTERNACH, *Vita Sanctae Hildergardis*, TRANS. PETER DRONKE FROM *Women Writers of the Middle Ages*

Opposite: One of the detailed and beautiful illustrations in the manuscript of Liber divinorum operum simplicis , *now in the State Library at Lucca.*

PEOPLE OFTEN SPEAK OF A TWELFTH-CENTURY renaissance – a great surge of intellectual and creative energy coinciding with dynamic changes in society, particularly in France. If there was indeed a twelfth-century Renaissance, then Hildegard of Bingen was a truly Renaissance woman. Her life as an abbess in Germany could have followed an established, traditional, and unremarkable path, but her uncontainable energy and creativity meant that she forged out a role for herself as a writer, composer, adviser on political affairs, mystic visionary and prophet. Her extraordinary assumption of autonomy and her refusal to submit to male ecclesiastical authority often landed her in trouble, but she was a skilful advocate, who managed to argue her way out of problems until the very end of her long and active life. Hildegard's achievements as a writer, both of visionary revelations and of scientific and medical treatises, are less well known than her talents as a composer of fine choral music, but perhaps, most fascinating of all, she can now be seen as a powerful feminist voice in what was very much a man's world.

*A German woodcut of
the Holy family escaping
to Egypt.*

Hildegard the Visionary

Hildegard was born in 1098, the tenth and youngest child of a noble family. Her parents dedicated her to a religious life at her birth. She was often ill and she was also imaginative and highly-strung. Several autobiographical passages about Hildegard's early life were included in her *Vita* (*Saint's Life*) by Theodoric of Echternach. She had received visions and divine revelations since the age of three but, with uncharacteristic timidity, she had kept them a secret:

> *And in the third year of my life I saw such a great brilliance that my soul trembled; yet because of my childish state I could not say anything about it. But in my eighth year I was offered to God, and till my fifteenth I saw many things, speaking of some of them in a simple way, ... Then I became aghast at myself... I was ignorant of many matters in the outside world, because of the frequent illnesses I suffered, from the time of my mother's milk up to then: it exhausted my body and drained my strength. Worn out by all this, I asked my nurse if she saw anything besides external things. "Nothing," she replied, for she saw nothing else. Then, seized with a great dread, I did not dare to disclose it to anyone; ... I blushed deeply and often I wept, and often I would gladly have kept silent, if I had been allowed to ... But a*

certain high-born woman, to whom I had been entrusted for my education, noticed this and disclosed it to a monk whom she knew.

The 'high-born woman' was Jutta, the daughter of Count Stephan of Spanheim. Although she was young and beautiful, she had committed herself to the very hard life of an anchoress. This meant that she would be enclosed in a cell attached to a church for the rest of her life, the door walled up, and her only communication with the outside world through one window. Her father built her a cell at Disibodenberg, where there was already a thriving Benedictine monastery. Hildegard's parents knew Count Stephan and may have been related to him; at any rate they made an agreement that the seven-year old Hildegard was to be enclosed with Jutta. It might seem barbaric to commit a small child, and one who suffered frequent illnesses, to being walled up in a cell with an older woman; but Hildegard spoke very highly of Jutta who was probably a kind and attentive teacher and guardian. She taught Hildegard to read, and may also have taught her music.

Given the amazing breadth and depth of Hildegard's later intellectual interests, it is likely that she was an outstandingly clever little girl, with a hungry appetite for knowledge – a joy to teach. The fame of Jutta and her pupil spread, causing other high-born ladies to join them and the cell expanded to become a small community of nuns with Jutta as its head. When Hildegard was fifteen years old she took her vows as a Benedictine nun, and by this time Disibodenberg was in effect a double monastery, with a smaller community of nuns attached (and subordinate) to the original community of monks.

Jutta died when Hildegard was thirty-eight years old. She was Jutta's natural successor and the nuns elected Hildegard as their abbess. She does not say very much about what she had been doing all this time, except that she had been receiving her visions all along and, eventually, had confided in Jutta about them.

Throughout her writings Hildegard herself often suggests a connection between her frequent bouts of illness and her experience of divine revelations. She does not often give us details of her illnesses, but they often coincided with major visions, and these she describes minutely. She is always adamant that, unlike other visionaries such as her contemporary Elisabeth of Schönau, she could experience her visions with an inner eye, without losing any of her external senses. She did not generally fall into a trance or lose consciousness of her surroundings. She always spoke of 'the living light':

I cannot say how or when I see it, but while I am experiencing it, all sorrow and all pain is lifted from me, so that I feel like an innocent girl, not like an old woman.

Hildegard describes a pattern in which a period of illness – in the early days especially often attributed by

The monastery at Disibodenberg where Hildegard first joined the anchoress Jutta of Spanheim in her cell at the age of eight.

HILDEGARD
of
❧ BINGEN ❧

her to suppressing her visions – is followed by an intense visionary experience, which gives her an extraordinary sense of well-being, insight, and power. Details of the visions themselves, in particular falling stars, concentric circles, and other lights that dazzle or blind her, first alerted the scholar Charles Singer in 1951 to identify the visions as a result of a migraine phenomenon known as 'scintillating scotomata', in which the sufferer experiences visual disturbances in the form of flickering, dazzling, moving light in geometric shapes. A recent excellent study by the scholar Sabina Flanagan compares Hildegard's detailed descriptions of her visions with medical descriptions of migraine attacks compiled by the psychiatrist Dr Oliver Sacks. He distinguished between 'common' and 'classic' migraine attacks. Classic migraines include symptoms of visual hallucinations and alterations in mood, levels of consciousness, muscular tone, perception and memory. He observed that some attacks passed through a 'crisis' of intense mental or physical activity, which brought them to an end, and that sufferers often had a 'rebound' after an attack, in which they felt better than before it. Sabina Flanagan concludes that from her childhood Hildegard had suffered from 'isolated migraine auras ... and common migraines', and, from the evidence in Hildegard's later writings, she suffered her first classic migraine in a phase of illness and vision in 1141. This phase changed the way Hildegard thought of her visions and was to force her eventually to make public what she had concealed for so many years. She tells us in the preface to *Scivias* (her first book of visions):

> *...the heavens opened and a blinding light of extreme brilliance flowed through my whole brain. And it ignited my heart and all my breast like a fire, not burning but warming ... and suddenly I understood the meaning of the interpretations of the books, that is to say, of the psalms, the Gospels, and other catholic books of the Old and New Testaments... But ... because of doubt and low self esteem, and because of various things that men said, for a long time I refused the command to write, not out of stubbornness but out of humility, until oppressed by the scourge of God, I fell into a sickness.*

It is clear that Hildegard was held back from writing her visions down by a powerful dread of being thought 'different' because of her unique inner vision. Although she might be certain in herself that her knowledge was God-given, others might conclude that it came from the devil. Writers who published bold and novel interpretations of great texts could be denounced as heretics and prosecuted by the Church. This happened to Peter Abelard, William of Conches, and Gilbert of Poitiers in Hildegard's lifetime.

She seems to have absorbed the medieval low opinion of women, in feeling it unseemly for a woman to presume to undertake the intellectual activity of theological writing. She refers to herself as a '*paupercula feminea forma*', a poor little womanly thing, emphasizing the contrast between her natural capacities and

ad exponendum ⁊ indocta ad scriben
dum ea dic ⁊ scribe illa ñ secdm os homi
nis. nec secdm intellectum humane ad
inuentionis nec secdm uoluntate huma
ne compositionis s; secdm id quod ea in
celestibus desup in mirabilibus dei uides ⁊ au
dis ea sic edisserendo pferens quemadmo
dum ⁊ auditor uerba pceptoris sui pcipi
ens ea secdm tenore locutionis illi ipso uo
lente ostendente ⁊ pcipiente ppalat. Sic
q ⁊ tu o homo. dic ea q uides ⁊ audis ⁊ scri
be ea non secdm te. nec secdm aliu homi
nem s; secundu uoluntate scientis uiden
tis ⁊ disponentis omnia in secretis miste
riorum suorum. Et iteru audiui uoce
de celo michi dicente. Dic q mirabilia
hec. ⁊ scribe ea hoc modo edocta ⁊ dic.

Factum e in millesimo centesimo
quadragesimo pmo filii dei ihu xpi
incarnationis anno. cu qdraginta duor
annor septe q; mensium eem maxime conisca
tionis igneu lum apto celo ueniens totu
cerebru meu transfudit. ⁊ totu cor totuq;
pectus meu uelut flamma ñ tam ar
dens s; calens ita inflammauit. ut sol
rem aliquam calefacit. sup quam radi
os suos ponit. Et repente intellectum
expositionis libror uidelicet psalterii
euuangelii ⁊ alior catholicor tam ue
teris quam noui testamenti uolumi
num sapiebam ñ aute inpretatio
nem uerbor textus eor nec diuisione

⁊ ecce quadra
gesimo tercio
temporalis cur
sus mei anno
cum celesti uisi
oni magno ti
more ⁊ tremu
la intentione inhererem uidi maxi
mu splendore in quo facta e uox
de celo ad me dicens. O homo fragi
lis ⁊ cinis cineris ⁊ putredo putredi
nis. dic ⁊ scribe q uides ⁊ audis. Sed
quia timida es ad loquendu ⁊ simplex

*Hildegard explaining her
visions to Volmar, her
trusted confessor.*

the glorious role God had bestowed on her, as the vessel for his divine revelations.
In an autobiographical passage from the *Vita*, Hildegard describes the events that
led to her decide she must write her visions down:

> ... *After [Jutta's] death, I kept seeing in this way till my fortieth year. Then
> in that same vision I was forced by a great pressure of pains to reveal what
> I had seen and heard. But I was very much afraid, and ashamed to tell what
> I had kept secret for so long ... I privately confided all this to a monk who
> was my magister ... Astonished, he told me to write these things down*

HILDEGARD
of
❦ BINGEN ❦

Hildegard did not illustrate her own works, but left detailed briefs for artists. This kind of picture, with flashing stars and shooting flames, first alerted scholars to the possibility that Hildegard's visions may have had a physiological origin and been symptoms of a migraine.

discreetly, till he could see what they were and what was their source. Then, realizing that they came from God, he pointed this out to his abbot, and from that time on he worked at this [writing down] with me, very eagerly.

In other words, Hildegard gradually overcame her fear of condemnation from others by seeking, and gaining, the approval of the male church hierarchy. The monk was Volmar, her teacher and confessor who later acted as Hildegard's secretary for many years, until his death in 1173. He was deeply impressed by Hildegard's visions and convinced that they had a divine and not a diabolical source. He gained the approval of Abbot Kuno of Disibodenberg for Hildegard to continue writing, and over the next ten years she completed *Scivias*, short for *Scito vias domini* or *Know the Ways of God*. Volmar must have made copies for circulation, including the Archbishop of Mainz, in whose diocese Disibodenberg was. Then Hildegard had a great stroke of good fortune. Pope Eugenius was attending the synod of Trier from November 1147 to February 1148, when Hildegard was still in the middle of writing *Scivias*. Eugenius sent a commission to Disibodenberg to investigate Hildegard. They were satisfied that she genuinely was the recipient of divine revelations, and brought back the first part of *Scivias*. According to the *Vita*, he took it into his own hands and read it aloud to the assembled archbishops and cardinals, before writing a letter to Hildegard commanding her to continue writing. This was the ultimate earthly seal of approval, and it was to have profound consequences for the rest of her life. The official acceptance of her divine authority gave her a formidable weapon; anyone who opposed her was thwarting the will of God.

Hildegard completed *Scivias* in 1151, and it made her something of a celebrity. The book itself is divided into three parts, each consisting of a series of visions and their detailed interpretations. The visions themselves cover many different subjects, but broadly they contain the knowledge needed by the individual soul to attain salvation. Hildegard included her views on sin, the fall of mankind from grace, the divinely ordained remedy for that fall in Christ's incarnation, the Church, envisaged as a beautiful and stately woman called Ecclesia, and contrasted with Synagoga (the Jewish religion), the nine orders of angels, the meaning of the Trinity, the sacraments, Christ's passion, resurrection and ascension into heaven, the virtues and vices, the end of the world and the Last Judgement, and finally a collection of Hildegard's songs and an early version of her musical play, *Ordo virtutum* (*Play of the Virtues*). Some of the visions are astonishingly bold in concept and scope, and Hildegard's idea of God's love for his creatures was radical; she saw this love and the power of creation as feminine, tender, and nurturing.

Scivias was an extraordinary achievement for a woman who had no formal education. It formed the basis for her growing reputation as 'the Rhenish sibyl', and her fame rapidly spread. She entered into correspondence with a large number of prominent people, including Pope Eugenius III and his successors Anastasius IV and Adrian IV, St Bernard of Clairvaux, Frederick Barbarossa, Conrad III, Henry II of England and his wife Eleanor of Aquitaine and Empress Irene of Byzantium. She later – and this was unheard of for a woman, in fact canon law forbade it – set off on a preaching tour of major German cities.

As Hildegard's writings were circulated, even before the completion of *Scivias*, her reputation attracted many patrons and new members to the Disibodenberg communities, and the monastery was continually being rebuilt to accommodate greater numbers. In 1148, after the papal endorsement of her prophetic role, and about eleven years after Hildegard had been elected abbess at Disibodenberg, she suddenly announced that God had commanded her to move herself and her nuns to a new foundation at Rupertsberg near Bingen. Rupertsberg did not appear at first to be a very promising site for the new nunnery. It had been left uncultivated

The Emperor Frederick Barbarossa, one the of many correspondendents who asked Hildegards's advice on a variety of topics.

HILDEGARD
of
❧ BINGEN ❧

St Bernard of Clairvaux,
who corresponded with
Hildegard and supported her
claim to be the recipient of
divine revelations.

for many years because of a defective water supply, despite being near the Rhine. But this was not such an obstacle as the opposition of Abbot Kuno of Disibodenberg to the move. Hildegard, however, was not going to allow anything to stand in the way of her plan. She refused to submit to his authority and, eventually he granted her permission to leave. Hildegard had her new nunnery built and moved her little community out there in around 1150, but at first the new convent found life very hard. Their makeshift wooden buildings were not so comfortable as the large stone-built foundation they had left, and one can imagine that some of her nuns, who had been brought up in wealthy households and were accustomed to their creature comforts, were not pleased at the move.

It was imperative that she gain control of the property and income that belonged to her community of nuns. Later she wrote an account of how she had browbeaten the abbot into submission. Her account is a mixture of absolute belief in her moral rectitude and a canny administrator's determination to have the business side of the arrangement legally and properly established:

Afterwards I returned under God's guidance to Disibodenberg ... and I made this proposal to all living there – that not only our place of residence, but all the real estate attached to it by deed of gift, should not remain with them but should be released to us. I then shared with the abbot what I had received in a true vision. The bright light speaks: 'You ought to be the father over ... the ghostly care of this spiritual nursery garden for my daughters. The gifts willed to them do not belong to you or to your brothers; on the contrary, your monastery should be their shelter.' But if you want to grow stubborn in your opposition and gnash your teeth against us, you ... are like the sons of Belial and you have not the justice of God before your eyes. Therefore, God's judgement will destroy you! When I, lowly creature that I am, had demanded from the abbot in these words to be made free of the place and to retain the endowments made to my daughters, all these things were granted me through a written contract in a legal codex. Everyone who saw, heard, or understood these things, both great and humble judged favourably of them so that it was clearly God's will that all this should be legally fixed in writing.

Hildegard also received permission to grant lay people the right to bury their dead in the cemetery at her convent, a practice that was usually accompanied by generous gifts to the foundation. So financial matters improved, and the new convent flourished, attracting further members. However fate was preparing a new blow for Hildegard.

Hildegard and Richardis

Hildegard had formed a very close friendship with one of her nuns, a young noblewoman called Richardis. Richardis had supported Hildegard throughout the move to Rupertsberg, had comforted her during some of her frequent illnesses, and had helped her to complete *Scivias*; but very soon after that, she was elected abbess of a convent at Bassum, and proposed to leave Rupertsberg to take up this appointment. Hildegard was deeply hurt at this defection and tried to thwart Richardis, suggesting that her election had been improper. Richardis's family was powerful and well-connected; her brother Hartwig was at this time the Archbishop

The convent at Rupertsberg before its destruction in the Thirty Years' War.

HILDEGARD
of
❦ BINGEN ❦

of Bremen; Bassum was in his diocese. Hildegard's desire to keep Richardis at her side made her show the worst side of her character.

Having failed to persuade Richardis herself, Hildegard then set about writing letters – to Richardis's mother, to Archbishop Henry of Mainz, to Archbishop Hartwig at Bremen, even to the Pope – pleading and threatening by turns, to persuade them to prevent Richardis from taking up her new post. They all took Richardis's part against her. In Hildegard's letter to the Marchioness of Stade, the mother of Richardis and grandmother of another girl named Adelheid, who also wanted to become an abbess, the tone is deeply personal:

> *I beg you, and urge you, not to perturb my soul so greatly as to draw bitter tears from my eyes and rend my heart with painful wounds, on account of my beloved daughters Richardis and Adelheid. Now I see them as in the dawn, glowing and adorned with virtues like pearls. Be careful lest their reason and their souls are removed from the height of that grace by your will, your advice, and your complicity. For the rank of abbess, that you want for them, is surely, surely, surely, not from God, and not conducive to the salvation of their souls.*

A woodcut of a medieval archbishop. The convent at Disibodenberg was, like most joint foundations, under the rule of the abbot. One of Hildegard's reasons for moving was probably her desire for independence from Abbot Kuno.

This personal appeal did not work, and the two girls accepted their new positions. Hildegard continued to protest about Richardis. The archbishop wrote her a letter announcing that he was sending an escort to fetch Richardis and accompany her to her new convent. He added that if Hildegard complied with his wishes he would show his pleasure, but that if she resisted, 'we will demand it again more forcefully, and we will not stop until you comply with our wishes in this matter'. Hildegard did not respond well to this mild threat. She assumed the full majesty of her role as God's mouthpiece and almost accused him of selling ecclesiastical offices.

Her threats and accusations fell on deaf ears. Hildegard, almost desperate, next addressed herself to Richardis's brother Hartwig, Archbishop of Bremen, blaming Abbot Kuno for confusing Richardis and making her lust for power. She begged Hartwig to make Richardis come back to her; she promised not to oppose her election as abbess at some future time, when it is God's will. But this appeal, too, was unavailing. Her final attempt to get her own way was by writing to Pope Eugenius himself. The Pope's reply is supremely tactful. He has nothing but good to say of Hildegard herself, but he gently reminds her that the devil longs to destroy those who are great, like Job; he says that the only ground on which he could compel Richardis to return would be that Bassum was not a monastery where the Benedictine rule was properly practised (and of course, it was).

Hildegard gave up trying to force Richardis to return to her, and wrote her a moving letter. She was momentarily assailed by doubt that she perceived the will of God correctly, and came to the conclusion that, instead of Richardis it was she herself who was being tested – God had punished her because she had loved Richardis too dearly. She suggests God caused Richardis's election in order to

Nuns hearing a sermon. In every convent a priest had to say mass and preach the sermon to the nuns. Nuns were more strictly enclosed than monks on the grounds that women were less able than men to resist temptation.

demonstrate to Hildegard the uncertainty of human relationships. Though she was now mourning the end of their close friendship, she blessed Richardis and wished her well in her new life. Her passionately strong feelings about Richardis are poignantly expressed:

> *And again I say, 'Woe is me, your mother, woe is me, daughter – why have you abandoned me like an orphan?' I loved the nobility of your conduct, the wisdom and purity of your soul, and your whole being, so much so that many people said: What are you doing? Now let everyone who has a sorrow like mine mourn with me – all who have ever, in the love of God, had such a high love in heart and mind for a human being as I for you – for one snatched away from them in a single moment, as you were from me.*

Sadly, this parting was a final one, for Richardis really was snatched away very soon after taking up her disputed post. Archbishop Hartwig wrote to Hildegard at the end of 1152 to tell her of his sister's unexpected death. He told Hildegard that she had died a holy death in the most perfect faith; but she had wept at the knowledge that she would never see Hildegard again. Hildegard must have found this assurance of Richardis's affection and regrets very comforting; she wrote back to Hartwig a letter full of forgiveness and love:

> *My soul was full of divine love for her, because the living light taught me to love her in a most powerful vision. Listen, God guarded her so jealously that worldly pleasure could not ensnare her: she struggled against it,*

HILDEGARD
of
❦ BINGEN ❦

A striking illustration from Scivias. *One of Hildegard's allegorical visions. The acceptance of her first visionary work,* Scivias, *gave Hildegard the authority to act with independence.*

though she grew like a flower in the beauty and glory and symphony of this world ... the world loved her beauty and glory and her wisdom, while she was alive corporeally. But God loved her more. Therefore he did not want to give his beloved to a rival lover, that is, the world ... Therefore I cast from my heart the pain you caused me in this matter of my daughter.

Richardis's death enabled Hildegard to revert to her opinion – that her election as abbess had been contrary to God's will. This justified Hildegard's desperate opposition, and probably helped her to recover from a wounding series of events, during which she had made a painful exhibition of her most personal feelings.

Hildegard the Scientist

Science as we know it did not exist in the Middle Ages. There was no appreciation of scientific method, in which new theories are tested and proved or disproved by experimentation. Instead, a largely unmerited respect for the 'authority' of previous writers, usually from classical antiquity, was the dominant motive for writers of scientific and medical treatises. Hildegard produced quite a large body of scientific and medical writing, and most of it is of this nature. However, she did also manage to introduce deductions she had made based on her own observations, and some of these are quite remarkable.

She wrote an encyclopedic compendium of information about the natural world, known as Physica, and a medical treatise, *Causae et curae* (*Causes and Cures*). Collectively these two works are called *Subtilitates diversarum naturarum creaturarum*, (*The Subtleties of the Diverse Natures of Created Things*). *Physica* is a more traditional collection of nine books containing other people's opinions about plants, the elements, trees, precious stones, fish, birds (including bats), animals, reptiles, and metals.

In the Middle Ages it was generally believed that all created things consisted of different proportions of the four basic elements (earth, air, fire and water), and therefore showed in differing degrees their chief properties, known as 'humours'. The quality of fire was 'choleric', i.e. hot, while air was dry, a humour known medically as 'sanguine', water was moist and anything in which this humour predominated was 'phlegmatic'; earth was cold, and the medical term for this was

A beautifully illuminated tenth-century Benedictine missal. The liturgy and the Benedictine daily offices were very important to Hildegard, who composed her own music for her nuns to sing.

97

HILDEGARD
of
❦ BINGEN ❦

'melancholic'. Medical theory, stated that all illnesses were due to an imbalance in a person's natural combination of these humours, and the remedy for any particular ailment was usually to swallow or apply to the skin something that had the opposite humour. For example, for a fever, caused by an excess of the hot or choleric humour, a medieval doctor would prescribe a medicine made out of something with the property of being 'cold', such as (according to Hildegard) the herb dornella (tormentil).

The first book, on plants, is by far the longest, and may contain some of the herbal recipes for medicines actually used by Hildegard and her nuns. (Hildegard's herbal remedies have formed the basis for a large alternative medicine industry in Germany today.) Some of her recommended remedies make use of ingredients that were easily accessible, such as the herb tansy. Following the premise that all created things were put on earth by God to be useful to man, Hildegard also suggests therapeutic uses for all the other things listed in the *Physica*. In many cases, the remedies she proposes can only have been theoretical at Rupertsberg as, for example, when she recommends cutting off a lion's ear and placing it over a deaf person's ear as a cure for deafness. However, she was accustomed to using earthworms which were a very useful ingredient in many remedies, mashed to a paste and mixed with other things.

In books six and seven of *Physica*, Hildegard states the humorous properties of birds and animals and also recommends whether they are good to eat, or suitable to make clothes out of, as well as their potential use in medicines. This section includes domestic animals, and one wonders under what circumstances Hildegard gained the knowledge that dogs are not good to eat!

Causae et curae is a much more discursive work, in which Hildegard discusses more generally her theory of nature, how the larger cosmos of the heavens and earth reflects, parallels, and is interdependent with the microcosm of man. She also states authoritatively her theory of the elements and humours:

> There are only four elements. There cannot be more than four or fewer. They consist of two kinds: upper and lower. The upper are celestial, the lower terrestrial. The creatures that live in the upper elements are insubstantial and are made of fire and air; those that move in the lower are bodies with tangible form, and consist of water and earth. For spirits are fiery and airy, but man is watery and earthy. When God created man, the earth from which he was formed was stuck together with water, and God put a fiery and airy breath of life into that form.

The greater part of *Causae et curae*, from Book two onwards, is devoted to a list of diseases, starting with the head and working downwards through the rest of the body, followed by a list of cures, described in somewhat more detail than in *Physica*. (The cure for baldness is to mash ashes from burned wheat straw into bear's grease, smear the result onto the head, and leave it there!)

‌⳿Uenales extant Londoñ. in Cimi
terio ſci Pauli ſub interſignio ſan =
cte Trinitatis. ⳿J henrico Jacobi.

*Left: A medieval woodcut of
St Benedict. Right: An
illustration of a monk from a
Benedictine songbook.
Hildegard and her nuns
followed the strict
Benedictine rules.*

Hildegard stamped *Causae et curae* with her own unique perspective. Much more than the *Physica, Causae et curae* contains insights and observations that genuinely seem to reflect Hildegard's experience and deductions. In particular, her remarks on human sexuality, and especially female sexuality, set Hildegard apart from her contemporaries. Hildegard describes the different kinds of sexual desire experienced by men and women:

> *A man's love ... is a blazing heat, like a fire on a blazing mountain, which can hardly be quenched, while hers is more like a wood-fire that is easy to quench: but a woman's love, in comparison with a man's, is like a sweet warmth coming from the sun, which brings forth fruits.*

Her opinion that a man's sexual desire was fiercer and hotter than a woman's is contrary to the received medical opinion throughout the Middle Ages that stated that women are more lustful than men, and less able to control their lust. Hildegard was quite unafraid of the idea of sexual pleasure, describing it in detail and in such a way as to emphasize its delight, while not harping on sinfulness. Consider this description of the sensations experienced by a woman during intercourse:

> *When a woman is making love with a man, a sense of heat in her brain, which brings with it sensual delight, communicates the taste of that delight*

HILDEGARD
of
❧ BINGEN ❧

during the act and summons forth the emission of the man's seed. And when the seed has fallen into its place, that vehement heat descending from her brain draws the seed to itself and holds it, and soon the woman's sexual organs contract, and all the parts that are ready to open up during the time of menstruation now close, in the same way as a strong man can hold something enclosed in his fist.

Presumably Hildegard, an elderly virgin, learned this account of the post-orgasmic spasm of the vaginal muscles from women outside the monastic community whom she was treating; or perhaps she simply questioned them in a spirit of enquiry!

Hildegard also formulated a theory, not at all in line with Church orthodoxy, that Adam and Eve had enjoyed sinless sexual relations in their pre-lapsarian innocence. According to her, sex in the Garden of Eden was a gift bestowed by God to give 'man the power of creation, so that through his love, which is woman, he could procreate children', but it was different from sex after the Fall, in that it was gentle and pure. After the Fall, sex became something hotter and coarser.

Hildegard theorized that there remains a memory in mankind of the sweetness of love-making before the Fall, which creates the sexual appetite, forever yearning for what it cannot have:

The great love that existed in Adam when Eve was created from him, and the sweetness of the sleep that he afterwards slept, were changed by his fault into a different kind of sweetness. And therefore because man still feels this great sweetness within himself, and is like a stag thirsting for the fountain, he races swiftly to the woman, and she to him — and she is like a threshing-floor pounded by his many strokes and made hot when the grains are threshed inside her.

Even this somewhat less romantic description of sex shows none of the distaste and disapproval (and sometimes even disgust) evinced by other celibate writers on the subject. Furthermore, Hildegard created a theory that the gender and the character of a child are predetermined by the feelings its parents have for each other at its conception, and by the potency of the man's semen.

The time at which the love-making occurs is significant, because the man's semen grows and declines in strength with the waxing and waning of the moon. At the end of *Causae et curae* Hildegard helpfully includes a kind of lunar calendar which enables parents to predict the character of their child according to the day of the lunar cycle on which it was conceived.

It would be inappropriate to try to assess Hildegard's contribution to the corpus of medieval scientific and medical

An illustration of one of Hildegard's striking visions.

works as a whole, but it is clear, particularly from the more speculative and original *Causae et curae*, that if she had lived in an age more accustomed to investigation, experiment and enquiry, she would have been an outstanding scientist, both because of her genuinely interested and curious mind, and her profound sympathy and respect for the human being as God's most wonderful work.

Hildegard the Abbess

Hildegard's huge creative output is all the more astounding when one reflects that she already had a very demanding full-time job being abbess of a new foundation. Rupertsberg, like the original house at Disibodenberg, was a Benedictine foundation, which meant that all its members observed the Benedictine Rule, with its eight long offices at set times of the day and night. In between these prayers and services, Hildegard had to discipline and advise her nuns at chapter, administrate supplies of food, clothing, and fuel, receive visitors, attend to legal business,

A typical illustration of a herb with medicinal properties. Hildegard practised herbal medicine.

HILDEGARD
of
❧ BINGEN ❧

Adam and Eve in the Garden of Eden.

Hildegard (in the bottom corner) receives a vision explaining the relationship of man to the universe.

supervise work on the convent land, and also the work of the lay brothers and sisters who probably did all the cooking and cleaning for the community. The Benedictine Rule prescribed a diet of vegetables, fruit, bread, beans, eggs, fish or cheese; monks and nuns were not allowed to eat the meat of quadrupeds, unless they were ill. Hildegard also notes that it is dangerous to drink water (this was probably quite true). Instead, she recommends beer and wine as more healthful drinks – especially beer which, she observes, brings colour to your cheeks and makes you plump.

Hildegard and the Benedictine Rule seem to have parted company over the clothing suitable for nuns. The object of the Rule was to promote humility, so fine clothes made from rich fabrics were not allowed, particularly for women, who were generally considered prone to vanity in their attire. Ordinarily Benedictine monks and nuns wore simple wool tunics, typically dyed black, with plain undergarments. Hildegard had her own ideas about this, to the scandal of some of her contemporaries. A fellow abbess named Tengswindis wrote Hildegard a rather sarcastic letter requesting her to explain two of her policies. Did Hildegard really allow her nuns, on feast days, to wear rings on their fingers, and elaborate veils and crowns on their heads? And what were Hildegard's reasons for only admitting girls of noble birth into her convent? Surely Hildegard could not but be aware that Our Lord chose people of humble birth, poor fishermen, to found his church? The heavy irony of the letter's close reeks of envy and spite:

> *Therefore we who are so insignificant, inwardly rejoicing at your advances, have decided to send our letter to your holiness, beseeching you most humbly and piously that you in your dignity do not disdain to reply to us very soon, so that our religious observance may be enriched by the authority of someone as great as yourself.*

Hildegard wrote a careful reply to this letter with its ironically disguised accusations. First, in the matter of the fine clothes and jewellery, she explained that although it is becoming for married women to comport themselves meekly and submissively, nuns in their celibacy are in a sense re-creating 'the simplicity and beautiful integrity of paradise', and therefore it is fitting for them to wear beautiful garments and ornaments like the brides of Christ that they are.

With regard to the accusation of only permitting girls of noble birth into her convent, Hildegard is also unrepentant. She makes reference to the perfectly accepted medieval world view of everything created by God being in its divinely appointed order, and then claims that it would be an unnatural outrage to mix up the different orders of society – if God put them all together there would be chaos. This too, she claims, is not what she herself says, but what God ('the living light') says.

Many people wrote to Hildegard asking her advice or asking her to predict the outcome of future events. She was asked her opinion of difficult points of theological theory by leading churchmen, and by other members of the monastic community. She began a correspondence with Frederick Barbarossa, sending him a letter of congratulation in 1152 on his becoming Holy Roman Emperor, but she wasn't afraid to admonish him in very direct language when, later on, after an unsatisfactory relationship with Pope Alexander III, he set up his own anti-pope: 'You are acting like an infant, and like an insane person.' When Frederick neglected to reply to this letter, he received an even sterner message from God via Hildegard: 'Woe, woe upon the evildoing of the unjust who scorn me!'

*A page from the manuscript
of Hildegard's own musical
compositions.*

Hildegard wrote her second book of visions and their explanations, *Liber vitae meritorum* (*Book of Life's Merits*) between about 1152 and 1161, and her third, her masterpiece the *Liber divinorum operum* (*Book of Divine Works*) between 1163 and 1174. In addition she wrote shorter pieces, such as the *Vita Sancti Disibodi* (*Life of St Disibod*) in between. The detailed and beautiful illustrations in the manuscript of *Liber divinorum operum*, now in the State Library at Lucca, were originally made at Rupertsberg. If Hildegard did not paint these herself she made very detailed briefs for the artists (presumably her nuns).

Hildegard the Composer

Music was very important to Hildegard and, in between carrying out her normal duties as abbess, conducting her extensive correspondence, and writing her great books, she also found time to compose a wonderful cycle of seventy-seven songs. They were for use in the daily offices or in the mass in her own community. Outside Germany she is, today, probably best known as a composer. This collection of religious music is known as the *Symphonia*; Hildegard referred to it as the 'symphony of the harmony of heavenly revelations', once again showing her inclination to create work with a large scope and a holistic viewpoint.

Some of the songs are obviously intended for the feast days of the many individual saints who were especially honoured at Rupertsberg. These included, of course, St Rupert and St Disibod. Besides these are included several songs on the Virgin Mary, John the Baptist, the Holy Spirit and the Trinity. The actual structure and arrangement of the cycle, the order in which Hildegard intended it to be performed, is a subject of scholarly dispute. As with Hildegard's other writings, the general tone of these songs is, unusually for the time, optimistic. She gives thanks, she remarks on the wonder of the incarnation, the wonderfulness of divine love, the deeply nurturing loving care of the Holy Spirit for sinful souls. She makes repeated use of several characteristic images – the dawn and sunrise, life-giving light, pure waters flowing, vivifying dew, greenness and blossoming flowers, crystals and jewels shining, sweet smells, flying up on the wings of God. They give the impression of a confident and joyful affirmation that virtue is strong and will triumph over evil, rather than the more prevalent medieval view that sin is the legacy of all flesh and most people will end up in hell. Musically, too, these songs are freer and more inventive than most Gregorian chants. Given that plainchant traditionally restricted the composer to the use of a single note – no tunes and no harmonies – Hildegard in her passion to praise God with the most beautiful music she could create, seized on the only possible sources of variation, and made dramatic use of 'neumes' in which a word is sung to a series of ascending or descending notes, and 'melismae' in which a single syllable is stretched over a sequence of many notes. These are devices for making plainchant more melodic.

Hildegard also wrote a musical play, the *Ordo virtutum*, or *Play of the Virtues*, in which personified virtues, together with prophets and patriarchs, battle with the Devil for possession of Anima, the soul. Hildegard designed costumes for her nuns to wear when they were performing this play which included white robes and crowns with symbols attached – this may have been what outraged Tengswindis.

For Hildegard perfect harmony served as an image of celestial bliss and this musical theme is reiterated frequently in her writings.

The Last Battle

In 1178, at the age of eighty, Hildegard once again defied the male ecclesiastical hierarchy in response to what her visions told her was the true will of God, making a really heroic stand against a cruel and, in her eyes, mistaken order. She had agreed to the burial in her convent cemetery at Rupertsberg of a local nobleman. This man had once been excommunicated, but Hildegard was satisfied that before he died he had been reconciled with the Church and had ended his life with all his sins confessed and absolved, and having received the sacrament. The clergy of Mainz, however, were

A vision from the Book of Divine Works, *now to be found in the State Library at Lucca.*

HILDEGARD
of
❦ BINGEN ❦

convinced that he had died excommunicate, and ordered Hildegard to have his body dug up and thrown out of the cemetery. If she refused to agree to this, she and all her nuns would be placed under an interdict, which meant that they would not be able to celebrate mass, receive any sacraments, or participate in the Benedictine daily offices. This was the most serious punishment that the Church could impose, short of trying someone for heresy.

Hildegard was determined to suffer this penalty, a dreadful privation for a religious community, because 'the living light' had told her that to give in to the order and allow the man's grave to be violated, would be disobeying God's will. Hildegard went further than simply refusing to comply with the order; she went into the graveyard and removed all distinctive marks from the grave, so that they

A painting of Emperor Frederick Barbarossa. His disagreements with the Pope about the role of ecclesiastical authority led to schism, war and one of Hildegard's most outspokenly critical letters.

could not identify it and send men to dig up the corpse in spite of her. However, she suffered particularly from the terms of the interdict that forbade the nuns to sing the divine office – singing had always been very important to her – and she begged the prelates in a letter to think again before continuing the ban on singing, because it was playing directly into Satan's hands, to forbid the recreation of heavenly harmonies that draw people's minds and souls to God. The prelates were unmoved. Hildegard wrote a second time to Archbishop Christian of Mainz. Finally, in March 1179, the archbishop replied, saying that he had instructed his clergy to lift the interdict if they were satisfied by the evidence of new witnesses as to the reconciliation of the dead man with the Church. Archbishop Philip of Cologne found a knight who said that he had been absolved at the same ceremony as the dead man, and the interdict was lifted. Hildegard had taken this courageous stand as a matter of conscience; she refused to be bullied into compliance with a course of action she knew was detestable and wrong.

Only six months later, on 17 September 1179, Hildegard died, loved and revered, among her beloved nuns. She was eighty-one years old. To those who knew her and in much of Germany where her fame had spread, she was now considered a saint, and a cult began in her honour. At this time the process of canonization was developing into something much more formal and bureaucratic than in previous years. The Pope had to issue a decree confirming sainthood, after a due inquiry into the manner of the subject's life, and miracles performed by them after death. The procedure was officially begun for Hildegard in 1227 and a document of the evidence for her sanctity submitted in 1233; but this was rejected and returned to the commission of enquiry for amendment. Another letter from Pope Innocent IV in 1243 requests the clergy of Mainz to re-submit the document, but they don't seem to have done so, and there is no record of Hildegard's official canonization. However, her local cult flourished and grew during the thirteenth and fourteenth centuries, and she was accepted by the general populace as a saint, whatever Rome said. Her church, containing her shrine and relics, can be seen today at Eibingen.

HILDEGARD
of
❧ BINGEN ❧

– V –
CHRISTINE de PISAN
c 1363–1429

> '*F*OR THE SAKE of strangers, let
> us celebrate the valiant Christine –
> Although death has snatched away her
> body, her name will live forever.
>
> MARTIN LE FRANC, *Champion of Ladies*, 1442

Opposite: Christine at work in her study, with her usual neat blue dress and her little white dog. This illustration is from a deluxe edition of Christine's complete works that she had made for Queen Isabeau in 1407.

CHRISTINE DE PISAN IS THE FIRST KNOWN professional woman writer in Europe. When she was left widowed in 1390 with three small children, a niece, and her mother to support, at the age of only twenty-five, she adopted the extraordinary and courageous course of trying to earn a living as a professional writer. In this she succeeded and by 1404 had attracted such a reputation as a woman of letters that no less a patron than Philip the Bold, Duke of Burgundy, commissioned her to write a biography of his dead brother, King Charles V. This was fame indeed, and success. But perhaps the most extraordinary thing about Christine from a modern point of view is that she refused to agree with the prevailing deeply misogynistic orthodoxy of almost all contemporary (male) writing. Christine dared to assert that women were just as capable of moral worth and heroic conduct as men, and contributed valiantly to the great intellectual debate of the day as the foremost apologist of feminine virtue in works such as *Letter to the God of Love*, *The Book of the City of Ladies*, and *The Treasury of the City of Ladies*.

CHRISTINE de ✣ PISAN ✣

Early Life

Although she spent most of her life in France, Christine de Pisan was Italian by birth. She was the daughter of Tommaso di Benvenuto da Pizzano, a noted academic in the fields of medicine and astrology. Tommaso had studied at the famous University of Bologna and in 1342 was elected to a chair in astrology. In 1357 he moved to Venice at the invitation of his older friend, Tommaso di Mondini da Forli, who had got him a job as a counsellor to the Republic with a very nice salary. He married his friend's daughter and, in about 1363 or 1364, the couple had a little girl, whom they named Cristina. Tommaso began buying estates around Bologna and seems to have planned to make his life there. But his fame had spread beyond Italy to the great courts of Europe, and in 1364 he received two invitations from foreign monarchs to take up a position as astrologer physician at their courts. Christine gives this account in her *Christine's Vision (Lavision Christine)*:

A somewhat less flattering depiction of Christine from an early printed edition of The City of Ladies, *showing her visited as she works at her desk by the allegorical personages Reason, Rectitude and Justice.*

... there came to him wonderful news in certain messages, ... from two very excellent kings who, because of the great fame of his expertise and learning, sent to him, each one praying and promising great salaries and emoluments that would be given to him, if he were willing to go to his court. One of these was the sovereign lord of all christian kings, the king of France, Charles the Wise, the Fifth of that name; and the other was the king of Hungary, the same who, on account of his merits and desserts, left behind him such a name that he is known as the Good king of Hungary. It was to consort with the most worthy, and also the desire to see the Schools of Paris, as well as the greatness of the French court, that he decided to come to the said king of France. He hoped for a limited time to see the king, to obey his commands, and to visit the said Schools, for the space of one year, and then to return to his wife and family, whom he ordained to remain on his properties and inheritances in Bologna the Fat ... (he) came to France, where he was very grandly received and honoured by the said wise King Charles. And, soon after having personal experience of his great learning and wisdom, (the king) established him as his special private counsellor and held him very dear. And this was so very agreeable to (the king) that (my father) could not get his permission to leave at the end of one year, as he wanted by all means to do. And so the king told him that at his own great expense, he would send to fetch (my father's) wife,

children, and family in order to spend ... their life close to him in France; and he promised him properties, rents, and annuities... Nonetheless, as my father was still hoping to return, he delayed this business for ... almost three years; but in the end he agreed that it should be done.

Christine was only four or five years old when she and her mother undertook the long journey from Bologna to Paris, across the Alps and up through France. There followed several years of prosperity, peace, and happiness. The King thought so highly of his astrologer-physician that he consulted him on all sorts of matters of state, and even took him away to the wars with him. King Charles was only thirty-two at this time, a thoughtful and scholarly person rather than a warrior. He gained a reputation for wisdom and statecraft; during his reign the kingdom enjoyed a respite from the ongoing catastrophes of the Hundred Years War with England, and began to recover some of its cultural pre-eminence. Both the King and his brothers, the Dukes of Burgundy and Berry, were great patrons of the arts, but the King was also interested in all branches of learning, and a great believer in what, for want of a better word, we might call right conduct. It is probably his influence that left Christine with her lasting preoccupation with order, propriety, and good sense that almost all her later works display.

Thomas was given a house in the city, a small country estate called Orsonville to the south-east of Paris, a salary of 100 francs a month, and gifts of books, clothes and food. Christine grew up in an atmosphere of harmony and plenty, and later wrote that she had been a happy child, always singing and laughing. She was a bright, clever little girl, who found it easier than her mother to learn the language and customs of their new country, but although she managed to pick up bits and pieces of knowledge from being much in the company of her father, she was given no formal education, because she was a girl. Christine was perfectly aware that an intelligent girl could benefit from education: 'If justice prevailed, a daughter would learn as much as a son' and she smarted at the unfairness of being denied access to learning because 'I had a real desire for it, and also great talent'. She did, however, learn to read and write, which was more than most girls managed and:

> *... I approached the age at which young girls are expected to marry. Though I was still quite young, there was no lack of knights, scholars, and others, wealthy and noble, and I was sought after by several. And this is the truth, not at all an idle boast. For the authority, the honour, and the great love that the king showed to my father was the reason for this, and not at all my own worth; just as my father considered him the most worthy*

Two lovers in the garden. This advises the reader to listen to others' troubles as you never know when you may need the favour returned.

who had the greatest learning and the best manners. He had his eye on a young graduate scholar, well born and from a noble family of Picardie, whose virtues outstripped his wealth, and whom he regarded as his own son … In this case I do not complain of fortune; he chose rightly, a man full of the most fitting and graceful qualities. As I have said many times, for my satisfaction I could not have wished for a better husband…
Christine's Vision, part III

The Perfect Marriage

The name of this charming young man was Etienne de Castel. She tells us that he had a beautiful figure as well as a handsome face, that in addition to the public virtues of wisdom, learning, and courtesy, he was also kind, affectionate, thoughtful and loyal. When they married, in 1379, he was twenty-four years old and she was fifteen. She later reported that on their wedding night he treated her with great gentleness and consideration; he 'did her no outrage', lest he should frighten her, and in the morning reassured his bashful bride with a hundred kisses, and told her that God had put him on earth only to be good to her.

For her part, she clearly adored him:

It seemed to me that he had no equal in this world, for my dearest wish could not have been for a person more wise, prudent, handsome, kind, or better than him in any way … We had so arranged our love and our two hearts that we had just one single entire will, whether in joy or sorrow, closer than brothers and sisters. His company was so pleasing to me that when he was near me there wasn't a woman alive more completely satisfied with every blessing. In every way within his power, with all sorts of pleasing trifles, comforts and delicacies, he made life easier for me.
The Path of Long Study, lines 78-97

The King gave Etienne the lucrative post of notary and secretary, which enabled the young couple to live in style, with four men and three maidservants to look after them. Christine always looked back to this time as one of perfect happiness.

Before long, however, the first of a succession of blows fell on the family:

the very excellent and wise prince, not aged by the course of nature, but at the very early age of forty four years, fell into a brief illness, from which he passed away. Alas, indeed and truly, it is often said that good things do not last long.
Christine's Vision, part III chapter 5

King Charles V was succeeded by his son Charles VI, a boy of twelve who did not share his father's tastes. With his employer's death, Thomas' prosperity vanished overnight. He remained at court, and he remained on the King's payroll, but he immediately ceased to be the King's very special private counsellor and friend:

CHRISTINE de ✤ PISAN ✤

A lover and his lady. This is the frontispiece to Christine's Book of 100 Ballades.

Now was the door to our misfortunes opened and I, being still youthful, was made to enter it ... my father had to do without his large pensions, amounting to more than 100 francs per month, and a scarcely smaller sum's worth of books and other gifts, and the expectation the said good king had given him of settling on him estates and other properties yielding an income of 500 pounds; the want of time remaining to the good king and the death that came for him too soon did not allow him to fulfill this promise. The promise did not bind the prince-governors; they retained him at court, but at wages adjusted downwards and poorly paid (i.e. late).
Christine' Vision part III chapter 5

Perhaps even more than the loss of income, the loss of Thomas' status, from cherished confidential counsellor to someone who only just appeared on the payroll, affected him deeply. He was also getting old – he was probably about sixty:

CHRISTINE de ❦ PISAN ❦

The time of his old age had already come, from which in a very short while afterwards he fell into a long infirmity and sickness in which many pains assailed him, among which must have been the needs of his dependents. ... keeping his sound understanding right up to the end, and acknowledging his creator like a true catholic, my beloved father passed away at the hour which he had predicted beforehand. Among the learned his reputation remained, that during his lifetime and for a hundred years before it no-one had seen a man of such excellent understanding and judgement in the mathematical sciences and in astrology.

Christine's Vision , part III chapter 5

Among his many outstanding qualities that his daughter mentions, was his great generosity to the poor; unfortunately this meant he had not much to leave to his family. Luckily Etienne was still employed and now became the head of the family. He did well under the new King. There was a regency under the Dukes of Burgundy and Bourbon, the King's uncles; they gathered a fine administration of talented and able men around them. Etienne was promoted and valued. He and Christine had a daughter in 1381, and a son, Jean, in 1385, and another son. These were happy years. Rising in prosperity, they moved in court circles and were personally acquainted with some of the greatest nobles of the realm.

Christine's later fame as an apologist for the female sex was grounded in a genuine liking and enthusiasm for the ladies of the court: Valentina Visconti, the wife of Louis of Orleans; Jeanne, the young wife of the middle-aged Duke of Berry, and Marie, his daughter; Marguerite, the wife of Bureau de la Rivière, the King's Chamberlain. Christine tells this charming story about Marguerite, which gives us a vivid glimpse into the kind of court social events attended by Christine.

This woodcut from Christine's Epitre d'Othea *warns the reader of the perils of boasting. Arachne claimed that she could spin and weave better than Pallas herself. Pallas, filled with anger, turned her into a spider.*

It happened one day that she attended a magnificent party given by the Duke of Anjou, ... As this young and beautiful lady was looking about her at all the noble knights present, she noticed that she could not see among them a very famous knight with a great reputation ... whose name was Messire Emenion de Pommiers. He was an old man, but she had never ceased to remember him because of his great goodness and valliance. She asked where that knight was, since she could not see him. She was told that he was in prison in the Chatelet, because he owed a debt of five hundred francs for travelling expenses undertaken when he was fighting. 'Ha!' said the noble lady, 'what a dreadful shame, that this kingdom should suffer such a man to be imprisoned for just one

hour for debt.' And so she took the rich and beautiful golden coronet that she wore on her head, and gave it to a messenger, saying, 'Give this coronet as security against his debt, get him set free and bring him here quickly!' and she put a wreath of flowers into her blonde hair instead. This was done, and she was much praised.
The Book of the City of Ladies

But all this was to change. Christine describes her misfortune using the very common medieval image of the fickle goddess Fortuna, imbuing her with a particularly vivid sense of her cruelty and envy:

> *Now my young husband had become the head of the family, a good, wise and prudent man, and very well beloved by the princes and by everyone who knew him. The status of my family was maintained by means of his sense and judgement; but soon Fortune made me descend to misery on her wheel; she wanted more than anything to cast me down to the lowest depth. She did not want me to enjoy any longer the company of that good man, ... (Fortune) snatched him away from me in the flower of his youth at the age of 34 years; and me, at the age of 25, she left burdened with three small children and a large household.*
> Christine's Vision, part III,

A woodcut showing Hector preparing to go into battle. His wife, Andromachne, dreamt that he would be killed, but he went to fight and perished.

Etienne had been accompanying the King on a visit to Beauvais when he became ill. We do not know exactly what he caught, but he died very suddenly. This was devastating for Christine. She remarks, and one can imagine her tortured by the fact, that she herself was not present at her husband's death; he was 'unaccompanied except by a few servants and in a strange household'. The suddenness and the shock of Etienne's death incapacitated Christine for a while:

> *It was truly a bitter thing to lose him whom I loved more than anything else in this world. I was utterly confused by grief and sorrow, and I became like a recluse, crushed, dejected, lonely, weary. I could not take a single step without having a tear in my eye, struggling with my mortal sorrow.*
> The Path of Long Study

The Valley of Tribulation

But she had no time to grieve; practical necessities forced her to take action. What was she to live on? How was she to feed and clothe her family? Besides her three small children, the eldest of whom was only eight, she had her mother, her two young brothers and a niece dependent on her. It was imperative to find out whether Etienne had left her any inheritance. And now it appears that this paragon of a husband did have one fault after all. He did not confide in Christine about his financial affairs; perhaps he thought she was too young and ignorant. She can't help denouncing the custom, even though she can't bring herself to criticize Etienne:

> *… and so I was not able to discover precisely the state of his business. For it was the usual custom of married men not to tell or clearly explain their affairs to their wives, and very often evil comes of this, as I know from experience. And really it is absolute nonsense, when women are not ninnies but are prudent and sensible. And I know perfectly well that not everything he had came to me. And now I was compelled to put my hands to work, that had been delicately and daintily nurtured; I had never learned to be the navigatrice of a ship becalmed in the sea*
> Christine's Vision, part III chapter 6

Christine had never missed an education more than in the following years. She was attempting to get hold of a piece of property that Etienne had bought to leave to her and the children, and to get the arrears of his salary paid by the King's exchequer. She immediately found herself 'surrounded on all sides by writs and pleas'; not only was it very difficult for her to claim what was her due, but all sorts of lying rogues popped out of the woodwork distraining on her for debts they falsely claimed Etienne had owed them. This was all very stressful for Christine:

> *… to my bitter grief I saw the time that I was pleading and defending myself in no less than four courts in Paris, and on my soul I swear to you that I was wrongfully oppressed by wicked men … they made it necessary for me to plead in court, although I hated it … I had to sue to them for my goods at very great cost and expense. It would be tedious to tell even the half of it; the extortion continued for more than fourteen years.*
> Christine's Vision , part III chapter 6

Christine had led a sheltered life, indulged and protected by her father and then her husband. She was unprepared for the unpleasantness of the business she had to undertake. She wept at the sight of her mother and her little children, trying to cope with their change in fortune; her feelings of helplessness and anxiety caused her to have panic attacks: 'in my lovely, well-made bed on bad nights I have many times felt great shudders'. Sometimes she got into debt and bailiffs were sent in.

> *God knows how my heart was wrung when executions were made against me, and even my little personal things … were taken away from me by sergeants — the loss itself was bad enough, but even more I dreaded the shame. But when it was necessary for me to borrow something, in order to escape a very much greater inconvenience (i.e. being imprisoned), good lord God, how ashamed and red-faced was the person who asked it of her friends!*
> Christine's Vision, part III chapter 6

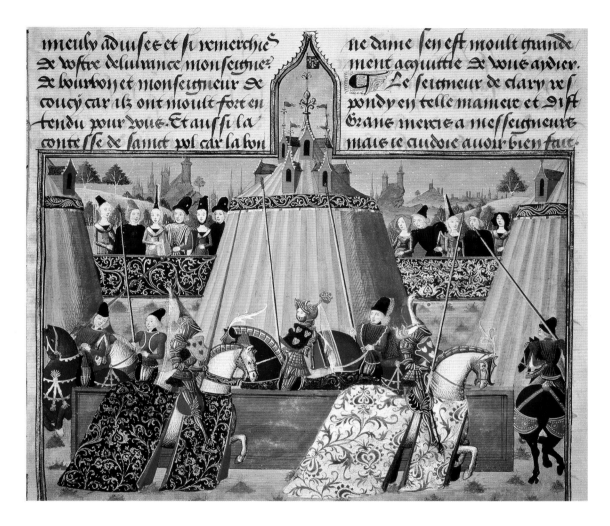

Christine also had to put up with a nasty form of sexual harassment. A respectable woman would not be seen out alone haunting the public rooms in the *Palais de Justice* as Christine was obliged to do, and it exposed her to leers and speculations as to the nature of her business from 'jokers or anyone stuffed with wine and greasy foods, at their ease':

> *Ah God, when I remember how many times I have had to wait all morning at the palace in winter, dying of the cold, looking out for those of my counsel to remind them to solicit my business, when many times I have heard in my ears the different conclusions and many strange remarks of those who followed me with their eyes, but it certainly hurt me deeply and made me very uneasy … what greater harm and misery can befall the innocent, what greater cause for impatience, than to hear oneself defamed without cause?*

Christine's Vision, part III chapter 6

The kind of glamorous social event attended by Christine during her marriage. This beautiful painting of a tournament comes from Christine's Book of 100 Ballades. *Note the watching crowd of ladies.*

CHRISTINE de ❦ PISAN ❧

Christine had made a decision after her husband had died, 'not forgetting my faith and the good love I had promised to him, I made a strong resolution never to have another'. It must have been particularly hurtful to her to find that 'it was said of me by the whole town that I was having a love affair... but I swear to you on my soul that that person did not know me ... I have marvelled many times from whom originated such words as those which were carried from mouth to mouth, saying that I had said Yes to him'. (Christine's Vision, part III chapter 6)

Worn out by the endless arguments and all the toing and froing in court, and by her natural reluctance to get embroiled any further, 'feeble in body and fearful by nature', Christine came to a compromise with the officials who were disputing her claim, and allowed them to keep part of the money in return for releasing the rest. All this left her with an indelible impression of how the odds were stacked against women who were trying to obtain justice, if they had no male protector, and she burned with indignation at the system whereby the most vulnerable and needy were the most preyed upon by greedy, corrupt bureaucrats.

It says a great deal for Christine's character that she persevered with her claims in spite of all these difficulties over a period of several years. In the end she received at least a partial payment of what was due to her; but it was too long in coming, and Christine had begun to write poetry in the early 1390s, at first therapeutically to relieve the fulness of her heart. She wrote ballads expressing how much she missed her husband and how awful life was without him. She then went on to write a whole series of love poems. These, she says, she wrote at the encouragement of her friends, for pleasure and not for profit. They were, however, a modest success, and established a reputation for Christine as a poetess. She very quickly seems to have had the idea of turning her gift to use, but she realized that if she was really going to embark on a serious attempt to earn money from writing, she must complete her education first.

The Path of Long Study

If Christine had been a man and had gone to university, she would have studied a formal course of rhetoric and logic, and would have been taught history and philosophy and how to express herself in writing. Instead, Christine had to teach herself. She had a study, where she kept the few books that she owned and books that she borrowed from the royal library, thanks to her friendship with the librarian Gilles Malet. She wrote in *Christine's Vision* how she had 'changed her life':

A fine fifteenth-century statue of King Charles V, 'the Wise', Christine's ideal monarch, which is now in the Louvre, Paris.

> *After these things, the greater part of my youth had passed already, and also the greater part of my external occupations, and I returned to the life which was by nature much more of a pleasure to me; that is, to sit alone and tranquil ... and the road of truth drew me to the path to which my own nature and the stars inclined me, and that is to a great love of study. Therefore I shut my gates – so that my mind should not be distracted by the vanity of external affairs – and I seized on these beautiful books and*

*volumes ... Thus like a child at first that learns his A, B, C, and D, I took
myself to ancient histories from the beginning of the world, the history of
the Jews, of the Assyrians, the principles of sovereignty, proceeding from
one to another, and working down to tales of the Franks and Bretons, and
several other histories ... and the more time I spent studying them, the
better I could understand them ... and my knowledge grew greater.*

In time, she progressed from merely reading histories and tales to appreciating the
beauties and subtleties of their composition, and to trying her hand at writing for
herself. Just as she had loved studying the works of others, she revelled in writing,
although she says she was initially doubtful about the amount of work involved.
She was encouraged, however, in a characteristically medieval manner, by the
personification of 'science de poesie' who told her:

*'Take the useful, and strike the subjects that I will give you on the anvil
til they are as hard as iron, so that no fire or anything else will be able to
destroy them. Consider if you forge wonderful creatures at the time when
you carry children in your belly, how you feel great agonies at giving*

*An early printed portrait of
Duke Philip 'the Bold' of
Burgundy, one of Christine's
most loyal and supportive
patrons, who commissioned
her to write a book
celebrating the character and
achievements of his brother,
the late King Charles V 'the
Wise' of France.*

CHRISTINE de ❧ PISAN ❧

birth. Now I want you to give birth to new volumes, which will present your mind to all future time, perpetually to the world, before the princes and the educated everywhere, which you will give birth to from your mind, in joy and delight; and the labour and travail will not prevent it, for just as a woman who has given birth forgets all her pain as soon as she hears her baby's cry, so you will forget the hard work of your labours on hearing the voice of your volumes.'

Christine began to write, as she puts it, 'pretty things, more frivolous' – her ballades, rondeaux and other poems – and, as the years passed and her skill and knowledge increased, she began to write 'in a changed style, of greater subtlety and deeper substance', concluding with justifiable pride that 'since the year 1394, when I began until this year, 1405, when still I have not ceased to write, I have made during this time 25 principal volumes, not including all my little poems, which all together make up about 70 quires in a great volume'.

Lady Authoress

The most obvious difference between creative writing in the Middle Ages and now is that medieval writers were quite comfortable admitting that 'there is nothing new under the sun'. Newness or originality were not valued. It was assumed that a writer would be using stories that already existed, indeed any writer worth his salt would be able to tell you exactly which classical author he got them from. Although almost all medieval writers were men, women too were at work in all areas of creative writing. Four of the six women in this book left written records of their thoughts and feelings and activities. Many women in the Church besides Hildegard of Bingen wrote letters, treatises, prayers and other devotional material – we have only heard of a tiny minority of them. There were several lady troubadours, known as 'trovairitz', and at least one major poetess working in the field of medieval romance – Marie de France, about whom, sadly, we know almost nothing besides her name. As Christine was really rather good, and sometimes excellent, and what is more, a woman, she gained a word-of-mouth reputation quite quickly. She had curiosity value. The nobles and wealthy beaurocrats who were for the most part her patrons were interested in owning copies of her work, and she managed to sustain quite a lucrative career over two decades from them.

Christine wrote in many forms and on many subjects, but she was particularly fond of the popular late medieval form of the allegorical dream-vision (like Dante's *Divine Comedy*, Langland's *Piers Plowman*, Chaucer's *Book of the Duchess and Parliament of Fowls*). She was a prolific writer. We don't have space here for a detailed account of all her works, as I want to concentrate on her chosen speciality as a defender of her sex, but a brief descriptive list will at least give some idea of the incredible range and scarcely less astonishing bulk of her output.

After her ballades and rondeaux, Christine wrote *Moral Teachings* and *Moral*

Proverbs, for her eldest son Jean when he went off to live in the household of the Earl of Salisbury in 1397. Then she wrote the *Letter to the God of Love* in 1399, which famously opened the great debate on *The Romance of the Rose*. In this poem she complains to the God of Love that many writers, including the author of *The Romance of the Rose*, were unfairly critical of women, and she makes a case for the virtues and good qualities of women in general which persuades the God of Love that they have been unfairly represented, so that he ends by ordering his officers to punish anyone who slanders and defames women, and ban them from his court.

Also in 1399 or 1400 she wrote *The Letter of the Goddess Othea*. This is another moral treatise, this time organized as a hundred rhymed tales illustrating a vice or virtue, purportedly told by Othea, goddess of prudence, with prose commentaries in Christine's own voice. This was probably also written for Jean, who by this time was back in France with his mother, the Earl of Salisbury meanwhile having been beheaded by new king Henry IV. Christine dedicated this very popular work to Louis, Duke of Orleans, who was then engaged in collecting his library, and had further copies made for presentation to the king, and the Dukes of Burgundy and Berry. She would have been given handsome presents by the recipients.

> *I made them a present as a novelty of some little tales and fables that were in my books on various subjects, which of their grace, like benign and humble princes they accepted them willingly and received them with joy; and since I was taking up an unusual thing, that a woman should write ... in a short time my said books were being talked about and carried to many different countries.*

Other nobles were also impressed with her work. King Henry IV, having very kindly offered to take her son Jean into his own household and bring him up, also offered her a place at his court; Christine, disapproving of the way he had come by his throne, rejected both offers. Gian Galeazzo, the Duke of Milan and father of Louis of Orleans's wife Valentina (who also had copies of Christine's books in her private library) sent ambassadors to Christine to ask her to live at his court. Christine gave this consideration, as Italy was her native country; but the Duke died in 1402, so she stayed in France.

Christine's daughter (her name is not recorded) had become a nun at the abbey of Poissy; In 1400 Christine wrote a poem called the *Book of the Tale of Poissy*, in which she tells of going to pay her a visit.

CHRISTINE
de
❧ PISAN ❧

John the Fearless, Duke of Burgundy (son of Philip the Bold) – also a patron of Christine, but as a man instrumental in driving France into the catastrophe of civil war, he attracted her criticism.

CHRISTINE
de
❦ PISAN ❦

It describes very charmingly a journey in springtime along the Seine and through the forest of Saint-Germain, and interestingly for modern readers, a detailed account of the life of a nun living in the convent, as told to Christine by the Prioress. Christine dedicated this poem to Jean de Werchin, the Seneschal of Hainault, a man with an excellent reputation as a chivalrous knight. He admired Christine's work and had asked her to write him a poem about a lovers' debate; Christine accordingly added two love stories to the end of her poem and sent it off to the Seneschal to adjudicate. He must have enjoyed this role, because she wrote another poem on the same subject, the *Book of the Three Judgements*, with three case histories, almost immediately afterwards. In 1401 she wrote a very witty, assured, and entertaining debate poem, *The Debate of the Two Lovers*, in which a sad and disappointed knight argues that love is a destructive and chaotic force that only brings unhappiness, and a cheerful and optimistic young squire counters that love is a source of great happiness and brings out the finest qualities of generosity and trust in people. The scene is a splendid party being given by Louis, Duke of Orleans; the poem is dedicated to him, and the debate submitted to him for judgement. Unfortunately there is no record of the judgements made by any of these dedicatees.

This was followed by a straightforward account of a platonic love affair between a married lady and a younger nobleman, which Christine says she wrote at the request of the young lord concerned; *The Duke of True Lovers*.

All the time that she was writing these shorter poems, Christine was also hard at work on a really major one – *The Book of the Changeableness of Fortune*. She began this in 1400 and finished it, some 23,636 lines later, in November 1403. As it was a subject close to her heart, much of the first book is autobiographical and gives some of the most appealing and intimate details of her early life and marriage, followed by the terrible loss of her husband and subsequent misfortunes. But she then moves outwards to consider the state of contemporary society in Italy and France, and then backwards in time to relate the history of the entire world - truly a mammoth task. Much of what she writes is, in the medieval fashion, plagiarised from other books, but it bears the stamp of Christine's own interests because she comments vigorously on the decline in moral standards among the ruling classes of France, and particularly on the lives of women.

Augustus receiving a vision of the Virgin and Child.

In 1403 she also wrote the beautiful pastoral, *The Shepherdess's Tale*, which incidentally contains much technical detail on the care of sheep as well as the main story, about a love affair between an innocent shepherdess and a noble lord; three religious poems, of which the second, *A Prayer on Our Lord*, is significant for its passionately imagined description of the agonies suffered by Christ during his torture and death; and *The Path of Long Study*, another poem containing vitally interesting autobiographical passages, but principally another dream-vision in which personified abstractions (Wisdom, Wealth, Nobility, Chivalry and Reason) debate who is best qualified to rule, in the course of which Christine manages to inject a lot of quite robust criticism of the power-hungry and rapacious nobles to whom the poem is dedicated.

Christine presented a copy of *The Book of the Changeableness of Fortune* to Duke Philip of Burgundy at New Year in 1404. The Duke was so impressed by it that he subsequently commissioned Christine to write a book celebrating the character and virtues of his dead brother, King Charles V. Christine accepted the commission very happily, as Charles V had always been her ideal of a good ruler, and she then wrote her first work in prose, *The Book of the Deeds and Good Customs of the Wise King Charles V*. Unfortunately Duke Philip died in April, before she had completed even the first section of her work; but she went on to finish it, and it has been invaluable to historians because it contains many personal anecdotes about the king and which otherwise would have been lost.

There followed in 1405 Christine's most important and individual work, *Christine's Vision*, again full of invaluable autobiographical details, but also a full-blown dream-vision in which she takes for her broader subject the sad state of her adopted country, France. In the third part, Christine visits an abbey ruled over by the abbess Dame Philosophy. Christine tells the story of her life – the same from which we have largely quoted here – in a rather whingey tone which shows that she blames Fortune for everything bad that has happened to her; Philosophy convinces her that Fortune is actually insignificant and powerless, that everything happens by the dispensation of God, and that Christine should be grateful for the good things He has given her, and stop whining about the painful events of the past.

Meanwhile in the real world relations between the king's brother Louis of Orleans and the new Duke of Burgundy, Jean, were rapidly deteriorating. Implacable in their rivalry for power during the illness of the King, they were both building up large armies, hiring mercenaries, dividing the country by factions. Orleans had the support of Queen Isabeau; Burgundy had taken the little Dauphin under his protection. Christine had a very prescient vision that this would all end in the misery and brutality of civil war (which it did, in 1411) and she now wrote an open letter to Queen Isabeau, begging her to use her influence over the princes in the cause of peace. She painted a grisly picture of the horrors of civil war, and also predicted that a foreign power would seize this opportunity to invade a France weakened by internal quarrels (which England did, in 1415), with the result that the best of the country's chivalry would perish (which it did, at Agincourt in 1415).

Her other works on general subjects are *The Wisdom of Man*, another moral treatise, *The Book of the Body Politic*, a treatise on the best way to order and govern an ideal state; *The Book of Feats of Arms and of Chivalry*, a treatise on chivalry with special reference to the proper conduct of warfare, seven allegorised psalms, *Lament on the Evils of the Civil War*, *The Book of Peace*, *Letter from the Prison of*

CHRISTINE de 🎕 PISAN 🎕.

This bold and striking image is an illustration from Epitre d'Othea.

Human Life, *Hours of Meditation on Our Lord*, and in addition her works on the subject of what we would broadly call feminism, – a spirited defence of her sex against the prevailing, almost universal misogyny of the time.

The Order of the Rose

The Romance of the Rose was one of the most famous and influential poems of the entire period of the later Middle Ages. It was an allegorical dream-vision, originally written by one Guillaume de Loris, who describes how he fell asleep and dreamed of entering a beautiful formal garden, at the centre of which was a lovely rose bush bearing one perfect, exquisite budding rose. The rose represents a lovely young virgin, with whom the narrator has fallen madly in love; in the allegory, his one desire is to penetrate the defences with which the Rose is surrounded, and pluck her. In this he is helped by personified abstractions such as Fair Welcome, Frankness, Pity, as well as the God of Love, and opposed by Danger, Jealousy, and Spite. Guillaume did not live to finish his poem, and forty years after his death it was continued by a very different author, Jean de Meun. In the latter's hands the *Romance of the Rose* ceased to be a delicate exploration of how to win a woman's affection and became a much more cynical account of how to get her into bed, liberally padded with the most outrageously misogynistic statements – all presented with quotes culled from classical authors and the Bible. Women, he claims, are all deceitful, even good ones; all are unstable and moody, naive and gullible, addicted to flattery and gossip, indiscreet, greedy, cunning, avaricious, spiteful.

Christine had suffered from the practical effects of the accepted low opinion of female virtue and intelligence and was unable to find them amusing. She had already dared to criticize Jean de Meun in her *L'Epistre au dieu d'amours* in 1399. Two years later she was having a literary discussion with Jean de Montreuil, the Provost of Lille in the course of which he had praised the *Romance of the Rose* as a work of genius. Christine disagreed with him, and what is more informed him that no less a person than Jean Gerson, the Chancellor of the University of Paris, also doubted that the poem was really a great masterpiece. De Montreuil subsequently wrote a letter to Gerson arguing that the *Romance* was excellent and not morally objectionable. He sent a copy of the letter to Christine; and though it was not addressed to her, she replied to it. Her letter was circulated, and the identity of its author made known. Christine was voicing a very unpopular viewpoint – de Meun was so revered that the poem was required reading for anyone with any pretensions to culture. Christine's counter to de Montreuil's letter was all that was mild and reasonable; de Meun was unfair because all women could not be as bad as he said; plainly many women were wise, intelligent, loving, and well-conducted. In addition de Meun denigrated marriage and recommended promiscuity.

Christine's letter provoked a little storm of controversy; and before very long it attracted a response from Gontier Col, secretary and later a general counsellor of the king. He asked her to send him a copy of the letter, so that he could leap to the defence of 'my master teacher Jean de Meun, true catholic solemn master and doctor in his time in holy theology and very profound and excellent philosophy'. His extraordinarily rude letter gives us some idea of what Christine was up against:

> *And in order to lead you to the real truth, and that you should know and be familiar with the works of the said de Meun, in order to give you something to write about if you write anything further against him, if that seems like a good idea to you or rather to your satellites, who in this deed have struck through you because they did not know how to or dare to touch him themselves, but they wanted to use you as their*

CHRISTINE
de
❦ PISAN ❧

The Roman moon goddess, Diana, smiting her worshippers with lunacy.

rain-cloak — for to say all this they must be more than just one woman ... I send you patently and speedily a treasure-trove compiled by him Sept articles de la foi, *a conventional religious treatise and if you do not withdraw and unsay what you have dared to charge, to correct, and to improve his words, then I trust in good and true justice, and that truth who does not cut corners will be with me, and however many weighty occupations I am at present engaged in and have been all this time, I shall undertake to support him against yours and whoever else's scribbles.*

A woodcut illustrating a medieval proverb. This was from Christine's book of moral advice to her son.

Christine sent him a copy of her letter, and two days later he wrote this:

To a woman of high understanding, Miss Christine. Because the divine Scripture teaches us that when we see a friend err or commit a fault, we ought to correct them, and at first we take them to one side and, if they are unwilling to amend after that, then we must correct them in front of other people; and if after that they are unwilling to correct their error, then one should make an example of them, like the publican; and because I love you loyally for your virtues and merits, I have first of all in my previous letter that I sent you exhorted, advised, and begged you to correct and amend yourself from the manifest error, folly and madness that has come upon you through presumption and overweening pride, like a woman governed by emotion. Do not be annoyed if I speak the truth about this matter. Following the divine commandment, and having compassion for you through charitable love, I counsel you and require you for the second time through this my memorandum that you should want to correct, unsay and amend your aforesaid error towards the very excellent and irreproachable doctor of holy divine scripture and high philosophy, whom you so horribly dare and presume to correct and reprove, and also against his true and loyal disciples Monsieur le prevost de Lille and myself and others - and confess your error. And we shall have pity on you and will place upon you by our mercy a salutary penance. And please answer this and my other letter and let me know your good will at your leisure and ease, before I set myself to refute your false (saving your reverence) writings that you have made about him. God wishes swiftly to lead your heart and your understanding to the true light and knowledge of truth; for it would be a pity if you remained any longer in such error under the shadows of ignorance.

Christine then responded with great spirit to this frightful, patronizing man:

To the very noble and confident person, Master Gontier Col ... you desired to have the copy of a little treatise in the form of a letter sent by me to the most solemn clerk Monseigneur the Provost of Lille ... explaining the opinion held by me, contrary to his, of the great praise that he attributed to the compilation of the Roman de la Rose *... and to be willing to fulfil your good commandment, I sent it to you upon which, ... moved by impatience you have written to me your two extremely insulting letters, reproaching my feminine sex which you call emotional by nature and moved by folly and presumption to dare to correct and reprove so high a doctor, such a graduate, and so solemn as you claim that author is. And for this you urge me that I should deny and repent, and that merciful compassion will be extended towards me or, if not, I will be made a public example of ... Ha, high and ingenious understanding, do not allow the cleverness of your mind to be held closed by your own will! Look straight, with the sight of the most sovereign Theologian, and you will not condemn so greatly what I have written, and you will consider the praise that they have given it is not misplaced ... And if you so despise my reasons for the littleness of my faculties, which you reproach me with by saying that I'm like a woman etc., then know for a truth that I do not consider this a crime or the least reproach, because of the comfort of the noble memory and continual new experience of the most wise and valiant ladies that have been and are fully worthy of praise and endowed with every virtue, whom I would much rather resemble than be enriched with every blessing of fortune. But still, if at all events you want to disparage my vehement reasons, please bear in mind that the little point of a pin or a knife can pierce a large bag full and inflated with all kinds of stuff. And do you not know that a little mouse can attack a great lion and in the end discomfit him? So do not think in any way that I shall be moved or shaken ... whatever coarse or loutish things you say to me when you're threatening me with your clever reasoning; such behaviour is commonly frightening to cowards. But finally, so that you can retain in brief what I have written at length and many times, I say directly, and in duplicate and triplicate, as many times as you like, that the said romance of the rose, notwithstanding there are good things in it ... but because human nature is more inclined to wickedness I say that it can only cause wicked and perverse exhortation to abominable morals, encouraging a dissolute life with doctrines full of deceit ... And all this I wish and dare to say and to hold to everywhere and before anyone, and I*

CHRISTINE de ❦ PISAN ❦.

A woodcut from Christine's Epitre d'Othea.

*appeal to the judgement of all just and sensible men, Theologians, true
Catholics and people of honest and wholesome life.*

That's telling him! Gontier Col must have been so stunned by this wonderfully
robust and uncowed response that he couldn't find anything more to say to her. But
the debate rumbled on; he gained support from his friends, and Christine began to
canvas her aristocratic patrons, including Queen Isabeau, to whom Christine sent
a copy of the whole correspondence with a note advising her of how she was
working hard to support and champion the reputation of the female sex. Then in
May 1402, Jean Gerson himself, the Chancellor of the University of Paris,
publicly declared his support for her by writing a treatise condemning the *Romance
of the Rose*. This brought Gontier Col's brother Pierre, a canon of Paris, out of the
woodwork, but as he did not dare to attack Gerson, he merely wrote some more
patronising and insolent abuse of Christine, along the same lines as his brother.
Christine responded to this with a very dignified and restrained letter, saying that
they will never agree about the poem, and everyone is entitled to his own opinion.
She does point out that more august personages than herself, such as Jean Gerson,
share her views, and that he really ought to attack them rather than her, since she
is 'nothing but a little cricket that rubs its wings together all day long, making a

*This beautiful illustration
from* Epitre d'Othea *shows
the goddess of Temperance
winding an ornate clock.*

This illustration, also from
Epitre d'Othea, *shows*
Christine giving a copy of
her work to the King.

little sound that is insignificant compared to the great song of the noble birds in the branches above'. Clearly now bored with the whole business, she ends her letter by saying that no matter what anyone else may write, she isn't going to say any more: 'What I have written is written'.

Christine now had a sense of mission – that she was the one who was in a position to redress the imbalance in the literary treatment of women Christine passionately wanted people to be fair in their assessment of women's characters and abilities; to instil and promote a reasonable respect for them. To do this it was not enough just to defend the reputation of women from attack, as she had done in the debate on the *Romance of the Rose*. She must present a positive model, to counteract the many negative ones. So she wrote another of her 'principal books', the longest and most ambitious in scope yet: *The City of Ladies*. Christine describes herself sitting in her study reading a volume of classical poetry, and wondering why so many of the poets and philosophers of the past present women in such a negative light. Can it really be true that all women are so hopelessly weak and vicious as they are portrayed? Perhaps God really did make them more evil than men. At this point three personified abstractions, Reason, Rectitude, and Justice, appear to

CHRISTINE de ❦ PISAN ❦

Christine to convince her of her error, and to commission her to write a work that will correct the wrong opinions about women that are so widely held. They begin to construct an allegorical 'city of ladies' – an ideal dwelling place in which to place the famous historical and mythical heroines whose stories form the bulk of the book. The three virtues tell her stories about outstanding women in every sphere of activity – female warriors among the Amazons, female rulers of great ability, female scientists and inventors; and most of all, women who exemplified every virtue. Christine wanted to make this a definitive collection of tales of good women. Among the familiar classical stories, Christine adds some fascinating anecdotes about contemporary women whom she knew including a woman named Anastaise, an artist who was so expert at illuminating manuscripts that she was the most highly paid and most sought after artist in Paris, as Christine knows from experience, having commissioned several works from her.

Christine then wrote *The Book of the Three Virtues* or as it's also known *The Treasury of the City of Ladies*, a treatise on how to become a really good woman, in the sense of a useful and respected member of society. It contains advice to women in all walks of life, starting with princesses and ending with the wives of the common people, and it is full of common sense that is obviously based on Christine's own experiences

After the completion of this book in 1406, Christine seems to have given herself some time off. Queen Isabeau requested a copy of her complete writings so Christine commissioned a handsome manuscript, filled with exquisite illustrations, many of which show Christine herself in her plain blue dress; it's likely that some of these were painted by the woman illustrator Anastaise, but as none are signed we can't be sure. Christine presented this to the queen in 1407 and received a handsome present for it. The manuscript is now in the British Library.

Christine was by now a well-known literary figure in Paris, and was presumably enjoying the fruits of her success. In 1409 she began her work on warfare, *The Book of Feats of Arms and Chivalry*, and in 1410 she wrote the *Lament on the Evils of the Civil War*, another anguished plea for the most powerful nobles to avert the coming catastrophe. (The civil war began officially in 1411).

Early in the year of 1418 Christine retired to live in an abbey, probably Poissy, where her daughter was a nun. There she wrote *Hours of Meditation on Our Lord*, but if the community had been hoping for further devotional works from Christine's scholarly pen, they were disappointed. Christine was silent for eleven years; then something happened that brought her out of her retirement with a resounding paean of joy: the sudden extraordinary career of Joan of Arc. In July 1429, only two weeks after the coronation of

This allegorical woodcut from Les Cent Histoires de Troyes *shows Achilles keeping a vigil over the tomb of the Amazon Queen, Penthesilea. He killed her in battle, then fell in love with her. This was probably meant as another warning to Christine's son.*

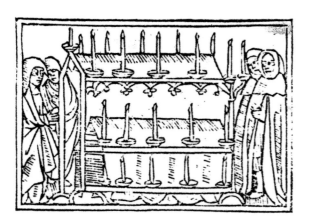

King Charles VII at Reims that Joan had done so much to bring about, Christine composed her final work, the *Hymn to Joan of Arc*. This united the two great themes that had preoccupied Christine for most of her mature writing career; the restoration of order and sanity to her adopted country, and the potential of women for virtuous and heroic conduct. Joan's victories seemed to Christine, as they did to many of her contemporaries, to be quite miraculous:

> *You who are a young maid,*
> *To whom God gives the strength and the power*
> *To be the Champion, and she*
> *Who gives to France the breast*
> *Of peace and sweet nourishing milk,*
> *And to overthrow the rebels,*
> *Truly you see an extraordinary thing! (ll 185-92)*

This allegorical woodcut is from Christine's Enseignements Moraux.

Here Christine manages in one stunning metaphor to put her finger succinctly on the enigma and the marvel of Joan of Arc, and also to sum up her own lifelong arguments in favour of recognizing the true value of the female sex. She recognizes that Joan is not merely a pseudo man, a soldier, bullying and swaggering and growing rich on the sufferings of others; Joan is actually motivated by a deep desire to put an end to the conflict, throw the English out of France, restore order and peace, make life tranquil and prosperous again. And this was a role she specifically claimed for women:

> *Ha! What an honour for the feminine sex!*
> *It's clear that God loves them. (ll 265-6)*

And there is a most moving resonance about the way in which France's first woman of letters opens her poem; speaking in her own voice and conscious of the fame she has achieved for herself after her years of work , she says "Je, Christine" greets and congratulates "Tu, Jehanne" – woman speaking to woman – self-taught scholar and author speaking to visionary warrior saint and heroine – an event unprecedented in the whole of European history up to that day.

This is the last we hear of Christine; the date of her death is unknown. Her work enjoyed considerable respect for at least a hundred years after her heyday, particularly in England, where translations of three of her works were some of the earliest printed books in English. After this she suffered an eclipse and, until recently, almost all her works were unpublished. Now, however, modern editions and translations are available, and we can once more feel that we are making the personal aquaintance of this most sympathetic pioneer of the feminist movement.

– VI –
❧ MARGARET PASTON ❧
1423–1484

> '*M*OTHER, SAVING YOUR pleasure, there
> needs no ambassadors between you and me;
> for there is neither wife nor other friend shall
> make me do what your commandment shall
> make me do, if I may have knowledge of it.
>
> ❧ JOHN PASTON III TO HIS MOTHER,
> MARGARET PASTON, CIRCA 1482

Opposite: The Four Conditions of Society: Nobility *by Jean Bourdichon showing a well-to-do family, like the Pastons. The accepted family heirarchy is suggested by their poses; the wife has a downcast gaze, but authority over her children.*

MARGARET PASTON WAS NOT AT ALL FAMOUS for her achievements during her lifetime. Posthumous fame has only come to her as a member of the Paston family who, over a period of 150 years, kept up a regular correspondence with each other that has preserved for us, in fascinating detail, the daily life and tribulations of a middle-class family in the mid-fifteenth century. Margaret's marriage was arranged by her family, but it seems to have been a long and happy one. She certainly identified with her husband's family interests to an extraordinary degree, and was trusted and relied on to manage the numerous family estates. Her role was indeed a most traditionally feminine one – that of an energetic, competent and reliable wife and mother, a role she performed outstandingly well. She was the most normal of the subjects of this book, the woman who deviated least from the way in which women were perceived at that time, as a subordinate partner of their men. Nevertheless, these turbulent times make this prosaic family saga fascinating, and we see Margaret violently ejected from besieged manor houses as well as ordering clothes and conducting marriage negotiations.

MARGARET ✣ PASTON ✣

Marriage among members of Margaret's class was largely a matter of complex legal and financial negotiations to support dynastic interests. Margaret, at least, does not seem to have been unhappy with her parent's choice.

The Young Bride

Margaret Paston was born Margaret Mautby, the daughter and heiress of a prominent Norfolk landowner. The first time we hear of her is in April 1440, when she was selected by Agnes and William Paston as a suitable bride for their eldest son John. The Pastons had been rising into property and gentility for a generation; they were ambitious, some might even say rapacious. William was a successful lawyer who had made an advantageous marriage to Agnes Berry, an heiress who brought him the estate of Horwellbury near Royston in Hertfordshire. William had been a steward of the Duke of Norfolk (1415), a Justice of the Peace (1418), a sergeant-at-law (1421), and was elected a Justice of the Common Bench (1429). He used his wealth shrewdly to buy more estates, and by 1440 was quite a considerable landowner. He also began the family habit of writing letters, as he was often away on business. Margaret, who would have been sixteen or seventeen at this time, brought more property to her husband. He was a student at Cambridge at the time of his marriage; his father was on the Bench in London, so Agnes wrote to him to report how the two young people liked each other on their first meeting:

> Agnes Paston to William Paston I, 20 April 1440
> *...I send you good tidings of the coming and the bringing home of the gentlewoman that you know of from Reedham this same night ... And as for the first acquaintance between John Paston and the said gentlewoman, she made him gentle cheer in gentle wise, and said he was verily your son. And so I hope there shall need no great treaty betwixt them.*

It seems strange that Margaret should not meet her betrothed, John, until all the arrangements for their wedding had been agreed by his parents and her grandfather, but this was not unusual for the time. The young people took to one another, for Agnes writes with satisfaction, and comments that there will need no 'great treaty' between them. Margaret appears to have been a good, obedient daughter and not at all displeased with her fate. The wedding was to take place in a short time. Brides did not wear white in the fifteenth century, but their best dress of whatever colour. Agnes goes on to say 'The parson...told me if you would buy her a gown, her mother would give thereto a goodly fur. The gown needeth for to be had, and of colour it would be a goodly blue or else a bright sanguine.'

The next time we hear of Margaret is in December 1441, when she writes to her husband. The letter is interesting, not least because it shows that pregnancy being thought indelicate and embarrassing was not a nineteenth-century idea:

> Margaret Paston to John Paston I, 14 December 1441
> *Right reverend and worshipful husband, I recommend me to you, desiring heartily to hear of your welfare, thanking you for the token that you sent me by Edmund Peres, praying you to know that my mother sent to my father to London for a gown cloth of musterdevillers (a kind of grey woollen cloth from the town of Mouster de Villers in Normandy) to make a gown of for me...As for the girdle that my father promised me... I pray you, if you dare take it upon you, that you will vouchsafe to have it made for when you come home; for I had never more need of one than I have now, for I am grown so 'slender' that I may not be girt in any girdle that I have but of one. Elizabeth Peverel (a midwife) has lain sick fifteen or sixteen weeks of the sciatica, but she sent my mother word by Kate (one of the Paston's servants) that she would come hither when God sent time, though she should be wheeled in a barrow. John of Damme (a family friend who held the manor of Sustead) was here, and my mother discovered me to him (i.e. told him she was pregnant); and he said ... he was not gladder of anything that he heard this twelve-month ... I can no longer live by my craft (i.e. disguising her pregnancy), I am discovered of all men that see me ... I pray you that you will wear the ring with the image of St Margaret that I sent you for a remembrance till you come home. You have left me such a remembrance that makes me to think upon you both day and night when I would sleep.*

The marriage bed. It is noticeable in medieval illustrations that, even when a bed contains a naked couple, they always have their hats on — a necessity in drafty, unheated bedrooms!

MARGARET
❧ PASTON ❧

Margaret has evidently fallen in love with her husband by this time, as her shyly affectionate tone and her desire that he will wear the ring she gave him testify. The baby, whose impending arrival Margaret was so anxious to conceal, was born some time before 15 April 1442 – a boy, named John (hereafter referred to as John II). John Paston I, meanwhile, graduated from Peterhouse and went to live in London, in the Inner Temple, furthering his studies in law. Margaret was left in Norfolk living with her parents-in-law (whom she refers to in her letters as her 'mother' and 'father'), mostly at their principal residence, the manor of Oxnead. Margaret could write but, as with other members of the family, dictated her letters to a secretary who could write much faster and more legibly than she could herself. Some time in 1443, John I fell seriously ill. Margaret wrote anxiously:

> Margaret Paston to John Paston I, 28 September 1443
>
> *Right worshipful husband, I recommend me to you, desiring heartily to hear of your welfare, thanking God for your amending of the great disease that you have had; and I thank you for the letter that you sent me, for by my troth my mother and I were not in heart's ease from the time that we knew of your sickness till we knew verily of your amending. My mother promised another image of wax of the weight of you to Our Lady of Walsingham, and she sent four nobles to the four orders of friars at Norwich to pray for you; and I have promised to go on pilgrimage to Walsingham and to St Leonard's for you. By my troth I had never so heavy a season as I had from the time that I knew of your sickness till I knew of your amending, and yet mine heart is in no great ease, nor shall not be till I know that you are truly well...I thankyou that you would vouchsafe to remember my girdle, and that you would write to me at this time, for I suppose the writing was none ease for you. Almighty God have you in his keeping and send you health. Written at Oxnead in right great haste on Saint Michael's Eve. Yours, M. Paston.*

This letter shows a typical approach to fifteenth-century piety. John's illness was life-threatening but, instead of turning to the medical profession, his wife and family committed themselves to a course of expensive religious acts. There is a strong sense that, if they put themselves to enough inconvenience and expense, John's health will return. It is often said that medieval people were 'more religious' than we are; but very often the their religious sensibility comes down to this sort of tit-for-tat superstition. When John had fully recovered, he and Margaret, as an act of thanks to God, paid for a very fine hammer-beam roof decorated with gorgeous carved angels in the newly rebuilt church of St Peter Hungate in Norwich. This church is now a museum, complete with the angel roof.

Margaret and John seem to have had a good marriage, a true partnership in which each was able to trust and rely upon the other. Margaret knew her place however, and accepted that her role was as a trusted but submissive deputy to her husband, not as an equal partner. There was affection between them; after almost twenty years of marriage, Margaret writes to her husband regretting that he won't be able to spend Christmas with her:

> Margaret Paston to John Paston I, 24 December 1459
> *I am sorry that you will not be at home for Christmas. I pray you that you will come as soon as you may; I shall think myself half a widow because you will not be at home ... God have you in his keeping. Written on Christmas Eve. By your M.P.*

However, a certain formality is always observed between them in their letters; she always addresses him as 'Right worshipful husband', and he only once unbent enough to address her as 'Mine own dear sovereign lady', after twenty five years of marriage. Regarding the business of the family they were usually of one mind, and it's clear from the letters how much of that business, in terms of running the household and the estates, devolved upon Margaret in John's frequent absences.

Managing the Estates

Margaret Paston was operating within the framework of a well established tradition in the societies of northern Europe. The duties of a wife in the nobility or landed gentry – families whose wealth was based on land holdings – included participation in the family business by managing the estates in her husband's

A lady hands a letter to her messenger. All Margaret's letters were written down for her by the family's confidential agents and delivered by hand by trusted couriers.

MARGARET ❦ PASTON ❦

A fashionably dressed young man rides off to seek his fortune in London, much as John Paston I, II and III must have done.

absence. She had to be a skilled administrator. There were manuals of household management – such as *Christine de Pisan's Book of the Three Virtues / Treasury of the City of Ladies* – which gave instructions on how to supervise servants and agricultural workers, how to calculate the revenues due on lands and service, how to oversee the harvest, negotiate the purchase of essential goods, sell crops and livestock, manage the stocks of food and drink, provide clothing and shoes for the household, and organize moving the household. Margaret had to do this in her husband's absence; she reports on her activities, negotiating with farmers, taking legal action against or trying to conciliate his opponents, holding meetings with tenants, instructing agents to buy and sell, to attend courts and to petition justices and lords on his behalf. He spent long periods in London; he was imprisoned three times and after his death, she continued her activities on behalf of their son. She reports regularly to John the sale of goods, the collection of rents, and so on.

Margaret Paston to John Paston I, 21 October 1460
I recommend me to you, praying you to know that the man of Knapton that oweth you money sent me this week 39 shillings and 8 pence, and as for the remnant of the money he hath promised to bring it at Whitsuntide. Thomas Bone hath sold all your wool here for 20 pence a stone, and good surety found to you therefor to be paid a Michaelmas next coming; and it is sold right well after that the wool was for the most part right feeble...Item, your mills at Hellesdon be let for 12 mark, and the miller to find the reparation; and Richard Calle hath let all your lands at Caister; but as for the Mautby lands, they be not let yet.

It also fell on Margaret to negotiate with tenants, and here one gets a sense that she often mediates between them and her husband, and is a more lenient landlord than he is inclined to be:

Margaret Paston to John Paston I, 8 April 1465

Item, there be divers of your tenantries at Mautby that had great need for to be repaired, and the tenants be so poor that they are not a power to repair them; wherefore if it like you I would that the marsh that Bridge had might be kept in your own hand this year, that the tenants might have rushes to repair their houses with. And also there is windfall wood at the manor that is of no great value that might help them towards the reparation, if it like you to let them have it that hath most need thereof.

She also often requests him to make purchases in London for her of rare goods which she cannot obtain in Norfolk:

Woodcuts of medieval estates. An able and hardworking wife, such as Margaret Paston, was essential to further the interests of an ambitious man who had to spend time away from home.

A medieval maid milking a cow. Cattle were very important, both for food and labour. During a dispute over a manor's ownership Margaret confiscated cattle belonging to the tenants as they were too frightened to pay their rent to her.

Margaret Paston to John Paston I, 1448
I pray you that you will vouchsafe to have bought for me 1lb of almonds and 1lb of sugar, and that you will have bought some frieƺe to make your children's gowns of. You shall have the best cheap and best choice of Hay's wife, as it is told me. And that you would buy a yard of broadcloth of black for an hood for me, of 44 pence or 4 shillings a yard, for (there) is neither good cloth nor good frieƺe in this town.

In other letters she requests either her husband or her son to buy in treacle, pepper, ginger, cloves, cinnamon, mace or rice, oranges and dates – spices were popular in the fifteenth century. She also gives instructions to lay in supplies of fish for Lent, and beef in the autumn to be salted down for the winter. Tenants on the Paston manors often pay their rents with grain or other foods; her servants trap rabbits and hares, or birds from the hedgerows – songbirds often featured on medieval dinner tables – in addition to the eggs and fowl provided by the dovecote and the poultry-yard. Margaret needed these resources because she had to provide for large numbers of people. Besides her family and household servants there were agents, bailiffs, chaplains, various legal representatives, plus a constant stream of visitors and their servants – friends of the family, business associates or other visitors. Households of this size had to maintain their own bakehouse and their own brewhouse to keep up with the quantities of loaves and ale consumed on a daily basis.

In addition, the provision of clothes for the household was a major task in the days when every garment worn by each member of the household had to be sewn by hand. She often requests John, and, in later years, her sons, to buy material for gowns, and accessories such as girdles, hats, gloves, shoes and hose (stockings) from London, where a better choice was available, and she is particularly careful to tell him what price he should expect to pay for these goods. This lettter is actually written by her third son Edmund II to her second son John III, but it was written from Norwich in November 1471 and this part is almost certainly from Margaret as she was with him when he wrote it.

> ... *buy me three yards of purple chamlet, price to the yard 4 shillings; a bonnet of deep murrey (i.e. mulberry, a deep purplish red), price 2 shillings and 4 pence; a hose-cloth of yellow-carsey of an ell, I believe it will cost 2 shillings; a girdle of plunket (grey-blue) ribbon, price 6 pence; four laces of silk, two of one colour and two of another, price 8 pence; three pairs of pattens ... I was wont to pay but twopence ha'penny for a pair, but I pray you let them not be left behind though I pay more...*

Houses also had to be furnished with sheets, blankets, pillows, coverlets, canopies and curtains – beds had to be snug and warm in big, drafty, unheated bedrooms.

There was scarcely a time when somebody wasn't taking legal action against the Pastons, and Margaret deputized for her husband in these more complex business affairs as well. Here she obtains a deed in connection with one of the manors whose ownership was disputed by the Duke of Suffolk:

Dinner in a medieval household. Well-to-do wives such as Margaret were responsible for providing dinner for any number of people, in addition to the immediate family, every day.

MARGARET ❧ PASTON ❧

A medieval banquet. Sweet and savoury dishes were served together at the medieval dinner table. Families displayed their wealth and status in the number and variety of dishes and the quality of servitors.

Margaret Paston to John Paston I, 8 April 1465.

Please you to wit that I send you a copy of a deed that John Edmonds of Taverham sent to me by the means of Dorlet. He told Dorlet that he had such a deed as he supposed that would do ease in proving the title that the Duke of Suffolk claimeth in Drayton. For the same deed that he sent me, the seal of arms is like unto the copy that I send you, and nothing like to the Duke of Suffolk's ancestors' ... the said Edmonds saith if he may find any other thing that may do you ease in that matter he will do his part

It was important to be on good terms with her tenants: where ownership of a manor was in dispute, the regular payment by them of their rents and dues was an important testimony to lordship. Margaret spent much time sending trusted men to talk to the tenants of disputed manors to gain their support. When they refused to pay their rent, she was not above seizing their cattle in lieu of payment:

Margaret Paston to John Paston I, 20 May 1465

...on Saturday last your servants Naunton, Wykes, and other were at Drayton, and there took a distress for the rent and farm that was to pay to the number of 77 neat (i.e. cattle), and so brought them home to Hellesdon and put them in the pinfold, and so kept them still there from the said Saturday morning into Monday at 3 o'clock in the afternoon.

However, these tenants were afraid to pay their rents to Paston because ownership of the manor was disputed by the Duke of Suffolk, a very powerful adversary. The

Duke's agents obtained a writ from the Sheriff of Norfolk which compelled Margaret, reluctantly, to give back the cattle. The poor tenants often got a raw deal in these disputes. The legal arguments often escalated into violence, and Margaret had need of every ounce of her energy and determination to battle, quite literally, against her husband's opponents on his behalf.

Defending the Properties

Margaret's duties were especially onerous because title to some of the estates claimed by the Paston family was disputed. This meant that in addition to the usual kind of tasks, Margaret participated in acrimonious court cases and, on more than one occasion, had to physically defend property from a violent assault.

The first time this happened was in 1448 over the manor of Gresham. This property had been bought from Thomas Chaucer by Margaret's father-in-law, but it was claimed by Robert Hungerford, Lord Moleyns. He sent his agents to claim rent from the tenants on the property in 1447; John Paston I made several unsuccessful legal appeals, and subsequently occupied the property from 6 October onwards. This meant that Margaret was living there, daily expecting an attack by Moleyns, while John was in London. Early in 1448 she wrote to him:

> I...pray you to get some crossbows, and windlasses to bend them with, and
> quarrel (i.e. crossbow bolts); for your houses here are so low that there may
> no man shoot out with any long bow, though we had never so much need.
> I suppose you should have such things of Sir John Fastolf if you would
> send to him. And also I would you should get two or three short poleaxes
> to keep doors with, and as many jacks, (i.e. long iron spikes) if you may.

We have no means of knowing whether John managed to provide this arsenal, but when the assault came, on 18 January, they were so terribly outnumbered that no amount of crossbows would have done any good. Poor Margaret and her men were violently and ignominiously ejected from the mansion, and a great deal of damage done to their property. John Paston submitted a petition to the King in 1449 describing what happened:

> on the 18th day of January last past, lord Moleyns sent to the said
> mansion a riotous people ... arrayed in manner of war, with cuirasses,
> coats of mail, steel helmets, glaives, bows, arrows, large shields, guns,
> pans with fire, long cromes (hooks) to draw down houses, ladders and
> picks with which they mined down the walls, and long trees with which
> they broke up the gates and doors, and so came into the said mansion, the
> wife of your beseecher at that time being therein, and twelve persons with
> her — the which persons they drove out of the mansion, and mined down
> the walls of the chamber wherein the wife of your beseecher was, and bare
> her out at the gates, and cut asunder the posts of the houses, and let them

MARGARET ❧ PASTON ❧

fall, and broke up all the chambers and coffers in the mansion, and rifled ... and bare away stuff, array, and money ... to the value of £200.

The manor was eventually restored in 1451, but Lord Moleyns was too powerful and well-connected to be compelled to pay compensation for the damage and thefts inflicted. However, Lord Moleyns' attention was soon diverted. He became Lord Hungerford in 1459 but came to a sticky end and was executed in 1464.

The second and third violent assaults came about through that same Sir John Fastolf mentioned by Margaret in her letter above. Fastolf was a famous military commander who had served with great distinction in France under Henry V and Henry VI and risen to be Governor of Anjou and Maine. He retired from active service in 1439, having acquired a huge fortune, and bought a lot of property in Norfolk. He seems to have been related to Margaret, and her husband John became a close friend of his. He himself was not a man to let an insult go unpunished, as witness his letter of 7 February 1455 to John Paston I:

> *...please you to know that I am advertised informed that at a dinner in Norwich, where as you and other gentlemen were present, that there were certain persons, gentlemen, which uttered scornful language of me, as in this wise, with more, saying, 'Ware thee, gossoon, ('lad', from the French garçon), ware, and go we to dinner, go we! Where? To Sir John Fastolf's, and there we shall well pay therefor.' What their meaning was I know well to no good intent to me ward. Wherefore, cousin, I pray you, as my trust is*

Armed soldiers attacking a castle. Margaret had to defend family properties from violent assaults on three occasions.

in you, that you give me knowledge by writing what gentlemen they be that had this report, with more, and what more gentlemen were present; as you would I should, and were my duty to do for you in semblable wise. And I shall keep your information in this matter secret, and with God's grace so purvey for them as they shall not all be well pleased. At such a time a man may know his friends and his foes asunder.

The consequence of losing: the enemy's men were allowed to loot and destroy valuables. Many victims of such assaults were never compensated.

John was evidently a satisfactory friend, for Sir John held him in 'great love and singular affection', and when he died in 1459 Fastolf left him three very rich manors, Hellesdon, Drayton and Caister, besides making him the principal executor of his will. This caused bad feeling among the other executors and legatees, and Paston was accused of exerting undue influence on the old soldier, and even of falsifying his will. His title to the estates was disputed and the legal tangle still unresolved at Paston's death in 1466. Hellesdon and Caister were seized by force from the Pastons; Hellesdon by the Duke of Suffolk in 1465 and Caister by the Duke of Norfolk in 1469. When the Duke of Suffolk raided Hellesdon, Margaret's husband was away in London, and when the Duke of Norfolk besieged Caister Castle, it was defended by her second son (John Paston III) while her elder son was in London. Margaret's letters to husband and son show the difficulties and dangers that had to be endured by a family like the Pastons when their opponents were wealthy, powerful, and influential noblemen such as the two dukes. Margaret's accounts of these events show how many public officials, as well as their tenants, were too intimidated by the threat of imprisonment, or even worse, from the Duke of Suffolk and his men to intervene on her behalf:

MARGARET ❧ PASTON ❧

An estate under siege. Margaret begged her husband to send crossbows to defend the house as the ceilings were too low for longbows to be drawn!

Margaret Paston to John Paston I, 17th October 1465

The Duke came to Norwich on Tuesday at 10 of the clock with the number of five hundred men, and he sent after the mayor and alderman with the sheriffs, desiring them in the King's name that they should take an inquiry of the constables of every ward within the city what men should have gone on your party to have helped or succoured your men at any time of these gatherings, and if any they could find, that they should take and arrest him and correct him ... and hereupon the mayor has arrested one that was with me called Robert Lovegold, brazier, and threatens him that he shall be hanged by the neck; wherefore I would that there might come down a writ to remove him ... he is right good and faithful unto you, and therefore I would he had help.

In addition to threatening Margaret's men, the Duke of Suffolk caused a great deal of damage to the manor and its buildings and contents. A lodge at Hellesdon was 'beaten down', the walls of the manor were severely broken, and even the church belonging to the estate was ransacked. During this assault the Duke and his men stole a large amount of valuable linen. From the church they robbed everything belonging to the Pastons and their tenants that had been put there for safe-keeping, including many valuable household goods, articles of lead, brass, pewter, and iron. Everything that they could not easily carry they smashed up. This action, however, turned public opinion against the Duke, and Margaret gleefully reported:

Margaret Paston to John I, 27 October 1465
I was at Hellesdon upon Thursday last past, and saw the place there, and in good faith there will no creature think how foully and horribly it is arrayed but if they saw it. There cometh much people daily to wonder thereupon, both of Norwich and other places, and they speak shamefully thereof. The Duke had been better than £1000 that it had never been done, and you have the more good will of the people that it is so foul done.

Later in the same letter, however, Margaret pleads with her husband to finish his business and come to help her, and it's clear how immensely stressful it was for her to have to deal with all this danger and aggression on a daily basis:

And at the reverence of God, speed your matters now, for it is too horrible a cost and trouble that we have now daily, and must have till it be otherwise; and your men dare not go about to gather up your livelihood, and we keep here daily more than three hundred persons for salvation of us and the place, for in very truth if the place had not been kept strong the Duke had come hither.

At one time the Pastons were on good terms with the Duke of Norfolk and had hoped to gain his support against the Duke of Suffolk, and even placed their second son, John III, in his household. None of this, however, prevented him from turning on them and seizing Caister Castle by force. This raid was even more serious, a

This was a dangerous time to be a prominent nobleman. However, country squires, such as the Pastons, were not important and were often pardonned for changes of allegiance.

full-scale siege with guns and armour, which resulted in the death of at least one of the defending party. Margaret wrote very anxiously to her elder son in London, trying to impress upon him the seriousness of the situation, and move him to take some action to help his besieged brother:

> Margaret Paston to John Paston II, 12 September 1469
> *I greet you well, letting you know that your brother and his fellowship stand in great jeopardy at Caister, and lack victual; and Daubeney and Berney are dead (actually only Daubeney was killed; Berney survived for many years and Margaret left him a bequest in her will), and divers others greatly hurt, and they lack gunpowder and arrows, and the place is sore broken by the guns of the other party; so that, unless they have hasty help, they are like to lose both their lives and the place, to the greatest rebuke that to you that ever came to any gentleman, for every man in this country marvels greatly that you suffer them to be so long in such great jeopardy without help or other remedy.*

Margaret was not at all unusual in her role as defender of the family estates; it was expected that a wife should look after her husband's and family's interests in this way. She was, however, unusual in being so energetic and determined, but there were as many 'women of character' – strong, able, authorititive – then as now, the only difference is that in medieval times marriage or the church offered the only career choices for such women to demonstrate their talents, and earn respect.

Parents and Children

Life was not always difficult for Margaret; there were other, pleasanter ways for her to express her dynastic concerns. She bore John at least seven children during their marriage: John II, John III, Margery, Edmond II, Walter, William III, and Anne (there may have been others who died in infancy). Much of Margaret's enormous energy was expended in trying to get one or other of them married. We can see from the letters how delicate and demanding the negotiations for an arranged marriage could be; of the many matches proposed in the letters only a fraction resulted in a marriage. For John III alone Margaret considered at least seven prospective brides before succeeding, finally, with Margery Brews.

John II, the eldest son and heir, was a bit of a hopeless case. He seems in many respects to have been a disappointment to his parents, and especially to Margaret. He did not share his parents' hunger for land and wealth, and he did not much like hard work. He preferred to live the agreeable life of a well-to-do courtier in London. His parents managed to get him a place at the court of King Edward IV in 1461. He was knighted in 1463 and became an MP in 1467-8, and a Justice of the Peace in 1469-70. He had a terrific reputation as a lady's man, in the sense of being flirtatious and agreeable company, but he never married, although he often got involved in match-making on other people's behalf and had an affair that

lasted for nine years which produced an illegitimate daughter. Perhaps this was the offence that caused a very serious quarrel with his father when he was twenty three. Paternal wrath was no trivial matter, even when a man was of age; John II was whisked away from the pleasures of the court, deposited in a lonely manor house in Norfolk, and forbidden to stir until his father forgave him. Margaret describes him as having been 'put out' of the house, which could mean physically ejected from it. Nowadays it would be almost unthinkable for a father to exert such authority over a grown-up son, but John II was evidently not a man to reject the financial security and social acceptability that being on good terms with his father gave him. He wrote to him on 5th March 1465, judging that a bit of grovelling might soften him.

Trouble at home: When Margaret's headstrong daughter was secretly betrothed to the family's bailiff, her blatant disregard for her parents' wishes caused outrage.

> *Right worshipful sir, in the most lowly wise I commend me to your good fatherhood, beseeching you of your blessing. Might it please your fatherhood to remember and consider the pain and heaviness that it hath been to me since your departing out of this country, here abiding till the*

MARGARET PASTON

The more conventional route to marriage; a protracted and complex business involving the settlement of money and property.

time it please you to show me grace, and till the time that by report my demeaning be to your pleasing; beseeching you to consider that I may not, nor have no means to, seek you as I ought to do, saving under this form ...wherefore I beseech you of your fatherly pity to tender the more this simple writing, as I shall out of doubt hereafter do what shall please you to the uttermost of my power and labour. And if there be any service that I may do, if it please you to command me, or if I may understand it, I will be as glad to do it as anything earthly.

Apparently this letter did not have the effect he desired, for next Margaret also sent a letter, pleading on his behalf:

Margaret Paston to John Paston I, 8 April 1965

*...I understand by John Pamping that you do not want your son to be taken
into your house, nor helped by you, till such time of year as he was put out
thereof...For God's sake, sir, have pity on him, and remember you it hath
been a long season since he had anything of you to help him with, and he
hath obeyed him to you, and will do at all times, and will do what he can
or may to have your good fatherhood...be you his good father and have a
fatherly heart to him; and I hope he shall ever know himself the better
hereafter, and be the more ware to eschew such things as should displease
you, and for to take heed at that should please you.*

This evidently did the trick, since John was back within the family fold by May. He
was much needed at the time, for this was during the thick of the dispute over
Hellesdon. Margaret wrote to her husband from the manor house there: '... I have
left John Paston the older at Caister to keep the place there, as Richard can tell you;
for I had liefer, if it pleased you, to be captainess here than at Caister.'

However, he remained very much in his father's bad graces; John I's next letter
to Margaret of 27 June 1465 shows that he had no doubt about his son's limitations:

*... as for your son: I let you know I wish he did well, but I understand in
him no disposition of policy nor of governance, as a man of the world ought
to do, but only liveth and ever hath, as a man dissolute, without any
provision; nor that he busieth himself nothing to understand such matters
as a man of livelihood must needs understand; ...but only I can think he
would dwell again in your house and mine, and there eat and drink and
sleep ... As for your son, you know well he never stood you nor me in profit,
ease, or help to the value of one groat ...*

Many twentieth-century parents of idle, feckless offspring can hear themselves in
this letter – the medieval equivalent of 'he thinks this house is a hotel', and it is
wonderfully typical that he refers to John II, with chauvinistic disapproval, as
'your son'. But Margaret herself found him disappointingly frivolous, slack about
the family business, lazy and extravagant. She wrote to John III after her husband's
death, complaining of John II's spendthrift habits, and saying 'it is a shame, and a
thing that is much spoken of in this country, that your father's gravestone is not
made ... There hath been much more spent in waste than should have made that.'
He himself seems, from his letters to his brother John III, to have been an easy-
going, good-humoured sort of chap, who liked to be on good terms with everyone.

John Paston III was a trouble to his parents in a different way. Margaret opened
negotiations for his betrothal to a number of young ladies, but they all failed for
one reason or another. He was an amorous man, and wrote to his brother John II
asking him to help get him 'a wife somewhere, for "melius est enim nubere quam
uri" (it is better to marry than to burn)'. At last a friend told him of a lady called
Margery Brews, daughter of Sir Thomas Brews of Topford, Norfolk, and he

Marriage was a sacrament which was not to be abused. When the Bishop of Norwich supported Margaret's daughter's betrothal, Margaret shut her daughter out of the house.

worked very hard to make this match work. His mother helped him, Margery's mother was also on his side, and Margery fell deeply in love with him; but her father, Sir Thomas, would not make over a sufficiently large sum as a dowry. For a while it seemed as if this would ruin the negotiations. Poor Margery wrote anxiously to her would-be husband:

> Margery Brews to John Paston III, February 1477
> *...my right well-beloved Valentine ... my lady my mother hath laboured the matter to my father full diligently, but she can get no more than you know of, for the which God knoweth I am full sorry. But if that you love me, as I trust verily that you do, you will not leave me therefore; for if that you had not half the livelihood that you have ...I would not forsake you ...my father will no more money part withal in that behalf but £100 and 50 mark...Wherefore, if you could be content with that good, and my poor person, I would be the merriest maiden on ground.*

All opposition was borne down, and the two were married later the same year.

Margaret's daughters were also a source of anxiety. The younger daughter Anne was at least a dutiful and obedient girl; she married William Yelverton in 1477. Margery, the older daughter, was a headstrong, determined girl, and did not get on with her authoritarian mother, who wrote in April 1469 to her son John II:

> *...I would you should purvey for your sister to be with my Lady of Oxford or with my Lady of Bedford or in some other worshipful place where as you think best, and I will help to her finding; for we be either of us weary of other. I shall tell you more when I speak with you.*

Margery resisted several attempts to marry her off – she had secretly entered into an engagement with Richard Calle, the family's trusted bailiff over two years before. Margery had waited until her father's death to tell her family. At that time such a betrothal, freely entered into by two adults, was almost as binding as the marriage ceremony itself. When Margery dropped this bombshell there was a huge family row. Her mother and brothers bullied her to see if she had spoken the words in a form that was not legally binding; they kept her virtually a prisoner. Only Richard Calle was on her side, he managed to smuggle a couple of letters in to her:

> *... this life that we lead now is neither pleasure to God nor to the world, considering the great bond of matrimony that is made betwixt us, and also the great love that hath been and as I trust yet is betwixt us, and as on my part never greater...*

Margaret then attempted to get her menfolk to put further pressure on her wayward daughter, but before she could do this the Bishop of Norwich insisted on examining her, to determine whether the words she had used 'made matrimony or not'. Margaret handed her over to the Bishop, but she made it plain that in her opinion and that of her fearsome mother-in-law, 'we could never understand by her saying...that either of them were bound to other, but that they might both choose.' The Bishop disagreed. Margery seeing her chance, spoke up boldly and 'said if those words made it not sure...that she would make it surer ere than she went thence; for she said she thought in her conscience she was bound, whatsoever the words were.' The Bishop then examined Richard Calle separately, and was unable to find a flaw in the words they had used to bind themselves to each other. Margaret reported to John Paston II on 10 September 1469:

Prominent noblemen paying homage to the King.

MARGARET ❧ PASTON ❧.

I was with my mother (Agnes) at her place when she was examined, and when I heard tell what her demeanour was I charged my servants that she should not be received in mine house. I had given her warning, she might have been ware afore if she had been gracious. And I sent to one or two more that they should not receive her if she came ... I pray you and require you that you take it not pensively, for I know well it goeth right near your heart, and so doth it to mine and to other; but remember you, and so do I, that we have lost of her but a whore, and set it the less to heart; for if she had been good, whatsoever she had been it should not have been as it is, for if he were dead at this hour she should never be at mine heart as she was.

To put her own daughter out on the street seems harsh, but was entirely acceptable, even quite moderate for the time. Margaret had the support of her mother-in-law, who had locked up her own daughter for refusing to marry an elderly widower, kept her solitary and beaten her 'sometimes twice in a day, and her head broken in two or three places'. Margery's brothers were also opposed to the match, for reasons of snobbery rather than outrage; John III wrote to John II in May 1469 to assure him that Richard Calle is lying when he says that he has John III's approval:

... I answered him that if my father, whom God absolve, were alive and hadconsented thereto, and my mother and you both, he should never have my good will for to make my sister to sell candle and mustard in Framlingham (Richard Calle came from Framlingham) and thus, with more which were too long to write to you, we departed. (May 1469)

Margery suffered all the blame – Richard Calle didn't even get the sack but, as a valued agent, continued to be employed by the family! In the end the two were married. Margery bore children, but died some time before 1479.

Margaret seems quite liberal in comparison with her mother-in-law. Agnes was probably more typical for believing in the efficacy of what seems to us, cruel treatment. Far from perceiving corporal punishment as wrong, it was seen as essential. Today we would agree that the absence of restraint doesn't teach the child proper values; it is the nature of the restraints that have changed. This was a more violent age than our own. The background to these family squabbles and disagreements over property was the Wars of the Roses; both the elder Paston brothers, started out on the side of Yorkist King Edward IV, but switched to the Lancastrian side and fought under the Earl of Warwick at the Battle of Barnet in 1471. In the battle John III was wounded but escaped. Edward won the battle and both sons were eventually pardoned. John III also fought under the Duke of Norfolk on the Yorkist side at the Battle of Bosworth in 1485, though Richard III had only pardonned him the previous year so he must have had another Lancastrian interlude. Having made his peace with King Henry VII, he was knighted in 1487, and accompanied the King on his invasion of France in 1492.

A contemporary illustration of a medieval town.

Margaret began to suffer serious illnesses at about the age of sixty, and was persuaded to make her will in February 1482. Much of Margaret's wealth is left in religious bequests, almost all of which are intended to benefit her soul and that of her husband. She was to be buried in her family church at Mautby, and left various funds for the church. Her gravestone should be carved with her family arms and the Paston arms, and the words 'In God is my trust.' She also gave detailed instructions about her funeral, in which twelve tenants were to stand by her coffin carrying torches, and candles were to be lit around the hearse. She left money for a large candle to be lit on her grave every Sunday and Holy Day for seven years during mass, for a mass-priest to say mass for her and for her husband for seven years, and for services to be said on the anniversary of her death for twelve years. She also donated two large and expensively produced mass books to the church. Other churches on her estates received gifts of vestments. She also left money for the lepers of Norwich and Yarmouth, and to the poor tenants on her estates.

Margaret left her family bequests of money, but also valuable personal items. She left her dead son's illegitimate daughter ten marks; she also left £20 to her daughter Margery's eldest child, so the two of them may have been reconciled, though this bequest was small in comparison to what she left to her other daughter. She also left bequests to all her servants. Any money left after all her wishes had been carried out was to be spent on 'deeds of mercy for my soul, my ancestors' souls, and all Christian souls'. She died on 4 November 1484. After her death the letter writing gradually declined and finally came to an end with the death of John Paston III in about 1503.

❧ FURTHER READING ❧

JOAN OF ARC
The most important source materials are: *The Trial of Jeanne d'Arc* edited and translated by W.P. Barrett (London 1931); *The Trial of Joan of Arc*, trans. W.S. Scott (London 1956); *The Retrial of Joan of Arc: The Evidence at the Trial for her Rehabilitation*, ed. Regine Pernoud, trans. J.M. Cohen (London 1955). For a general examination of Joan's life and her significance, see the fascinating study *Joan of Arc, the Image of Female Heroism* by Marina Warner (London 1981).

ELEANOR OF AQUITAINE
There are two very good general books about Eleanor; *Eleanor of Aquitaine, Queen and Legend* by D.D.R. Owen (Oxford 1993) and *Eleanor of Aquitaine* by Marion Meade (London 1977) – both quote from medieval-chronicle sources and have excellent bibliographies.

MARGERY KEMPE
Margery's autobiography, *The Book of Margery Kempe*, is now available in a modern English version in the Penguin Classics, translated and edited by Barry Windeatt (London 1985); the original Middle-English text can be found the *Boke of Margery Kempe*, Early English Text Society o.s. 212. 1940, ed. S.B. Meech and H.E. Allen. A good general book about her is *Margery Kempe of Lynne and Medieval England* by Margaret Gallyon (Norwich 1995).

HILDEGARD OF BINGEN
Hildegard wrote in Latin, and so far there are no English translations of her major works generally available. Translations of some of her letters, and autobiographical passages in her Vita are given in *Women Writers of the Middle Ages* by Peter Dronke (Cambridge 1984), and in *Hildegard of Bingen, A Visionary Life* by Sabina Flanagan (London 1989). Her Latin works can all be found in *Patrologiae Cursus Completus, serie Latina* vol. 197. ed. J.P. Migne (Paris 1841-64), or in *Sanctae Hildegardis Opera* ed. J.B. Pitra (Monte Cassino, 1882)

CHRISTINE DE PISAN
There is a good modern translation of *The Treasury of the City of Ladies* by Sarah Lawson in the *Penguin Classics* series (London 1985), and of *The City of Ladies* by Earl Jeffery Richards (New York, 1982, London 1983). Two general books are *Christine de Pizan: Her life and works* by Charity Cannon Willard (New York 1984) and *The Order of the Rose: the Life and Ideas of Christine de Pizan* by Enid McLeod (London 1976).

MARGARET PASTON
A good selection of the Paston letters with modern-English spelling is *The Paston letters*, ed. Norman Davis in the *World Classics* series (Oxford 1963) with an introduction, notes and a glossary.

❦ INDEX ❦

❦ INDEX ❧

PICTURE CREDITS